"A delight to read. . . . She writes of having babies at an 'advanced maternal age,' pursuing an academic career in a decidedly anti-Christian professional environment, trying to figure out how to juggle teaching with writing and family, and other day-to-day traumas of life, large and small. . . . She writes sweetly and earnestly, like a wise child. Or perhaps like the wise old woman of God that she hopes someday to become which, I'd argue, she already is."

Patty Kirk, author of *The Easy Burden of Pleasing God*

"Carolyn Weber lives gracefully and writes elegantly. Her poetic eyes search beneath the surface, unearthing delightful insights missed by those in a hurry. *Holy Is the Day* is a call to see God and latch onto him, so he takes us through the day as he envisions it. This is a beautiful book that spoke to my heart and changed my day."

Randy Alcorn, author of *If God Is Good* and *Deception*

"Life and death, sorrow and joy. Waves of life that roll into Carolyn Weber's life are beautifully, soulfully examined. The author's story is meditatively interwoven with Scripture's story, not to hand us answers, but to offer us hope. The book is lovingly and honestly crafted. Read this one carefully as it is a gift from a heart that has grown in wisdom."

Rick Lewis, Logos Bookstore, Dallas, Texas

"I could not put *Holy Is the Day* down! Right from her opening story, Weber hooks us with her luscious use of language and reels us close with her insights and stories, all keenly crafted to help open our eyes to see God at work and present in our days. A beautiful read."

Caryn Rivadeneira, author of *Broke* and *Grumble Hallelujah*

IVP *Crescendo*
COURAGE. CONFIDENCE. CALLING.

Some voices challenge us. Others support or encourage us. Voices can move us to change our minds, draw close to God, discover a new spiritual gift. The voices of others are shaping who we are.

The voices behind IVP Crescendo join together to draw us into God's story. We'll discover God's work around the globe even as we learn to love the people around the corner. We'll have opportunity to heal our places of pain. We'll discover new ways to love our families. We'll hear God's voice speaking into our lives as we discover new places of influence.

IVP Crescendo invites you to join in the rising chorus

- *to listen to the voices of others*
- *to hear the voice of God*
- *and to grow your own voice in*

COURAGE. CONFIDENCE. CALLING.

ivpress.com/crescendo
ivpress.com/crescendo-social

holy is the day

Living in the Gift of the Present

CAROLYN WEBER

IVP Books

An imprint of InterVarsity Press
Downers Grove, Illinois

InterVarsity Press
P.O. Box 1400, Downers Grove, IL 60515-1426
World Wide Web: www.ivpress.com
Email: email@ivpress.com

InterVarsity Press® is the book-publishing division of InterVarsity Christian Fellowship/USA®, a movement of students and faculty active on campus at hundreds of universities, colleges and schools of nursing in the United States of America, and a member movement of the International Fellowship of Evangelical Students. For information about local and regional activities, write Public Relations Dept., InterVarsity Christian Fellowship/USA, 6400 Schroeder Rd., P.O. Box 7895, Madison, WI 53707-7895, or visit the IVCF website at www.intervarsity.org.

All Scripture quotations, unless otherwise indicated, are taken from THE HOLY BIBLE, NEW INTERNATIONAL VERSION®, NIV® Copyright © 1973, 1978, 1984, 2011 by Biblica, Inc.™ Used by permission. All rights reserved worldwide.

While all stories in this book are true, some names and identifying information in this book have been changed to protect the privacy of the individuals involved.

Excerpt from "Carpe Diem" from Message in a Bottle by Ann Schultz. ©2010 by Ann Schultz. Reprinted by permission of Madonna Living Community and Foundation in Rochester, Minnesota, an affiliate of the Benedictine Health System, and the family of Ann Schultz.

Cover design: Cindy Kiple
Interior design: Beth Hagenberg
Image: © Martin Poole/Glow Images

ISBN 978-0-8308-4307-7 (print)
ISBN 978-0-8308-9575-5 (digital)

Printed in the United States of America ∞

Library of Congress Cataloging-in-Publication Data

Weber, Carolyn A.
  Holy is the day : the gift of the present / Carolyn A. Weber.
      pages cm
  Includes bibliographical references.
  ISBN 978-0-8308-4307-7 (pbk. : alk. paper)
  1. Christain life. I. Title.
  BV4501.3.W3925 2013
  248.4—dc23

                                                                    2013023999

P   21   20   19   18   17   16   15   14   13   12   11   10   9   8   7   6   5   4   3   2

Y   31   30   29   28   27   26   25   24   23   22   21   20   19   18   17   16   15   14

For the good folks of Westmont College—

Thank you for filling my well.

Contents

Acknowledgments

Since this project was the result of a leap with faith, I wish to thank those who launched me and those who caught me.

This starts with my church families on both sides of the border, so to speak: Montecito Covenant Church and the Westmont Community in Santa Barbara, California, USA, and Village Green Community Church in London, Ontario, Canada. In particular, warmest thanks to Pastor Don Johnson and his wife, Martha, and to Pastor Jon Korkidakis and his wife, Darlene. And to Diana and Dick Trautwein—how we miss the embrace of your home.

Cheers to my u-turn friends near and far who kept me afloat through the lived-out laughter and tears of this manuscript. You are women extraordinaire: Lisa Holmlund, Tabitha Elwood, Colleen Stelmaszek, Pilar Arsenec, Liz Adams, Nicole St John, Sarah Ristine, Charlene Mertens. And of course to Mary-Antoinette Smith, whose smile I feel over the miles whenever I write.

Much gratitude to my agent, Mark Sweeney, and his wife, Janet, for their genuine care. And to Jeff Crosby and Cindy Bunch of IVP, for their belief in and support of this project.

To the members of the Westmont English department I met

during my time there, your names alone conjure such a special season for me. Thank you for welcoming me in and lifting me up: Randy VanderMey, Paul Willis, Paul Delaney, Elizabeth Hess, Sarah Skripsky, Jamie Friedman, Cheri Larsen Hoeckley, Stephan Cook, Gregory Orfalea and Elaine Yochum. And a special dose of Canadian love (eh!) to Professor Emeritus John Sider and his wife, Anna, whose example and provision in myriad ways provide a constant reminder of the dear.

For my Pacific Northwest and Southern Ontario family, I give thanks, too: you have gifted me with your presence during the writing of this life as praise.

Victoria, Byron, William and now little Kingsley—you fill me with joy unspeakable.

Finally, my Kent, thank you for always holding my hand. And for doing so a little tighter when we leap.

Preface

My journey began on an early autumn morning back in Seattle as I gazed at Montlake Bridge, still suspended in the open position over the canal. I realized this would probably be the day. But as is our tendency with most every day, I just didn't realize what kind of holy day it would be.

Sunbeams through the old lead windows cast triangular rainbows across the room that morning. Something had changed over the course of the last few days. At first it was subtle. Slightly less energy, slightly more breathlessness when climbing the stairs all the way to top of our house with the laundry basket. Then the Braxton Hicks contractions came on, especially at night. Sometimes so strongly I'd begin counting in between, just to be sure.

Lying in the dark, I'd imagine my boys' faces, imagine their tiny limbs, washed and then swaddled. Always hungry, I'd imagine what was on the hospital menu. But then the contractions would fragment, thwarting any attempt at regular monitoring. And then they would subside altogether, leaving me tired from lack of sleep, but also tired from the worn-out waiting. I was full term, actually beyond, for twins—well into my thirty-ninth week now. But the suitcase all ready for the hospital would sit untouched, and dawn's rosy fingers would reach over the mountain range. I would arise and make coffee. A new morning.

None of these details concerned my daughter much; rather, sea-barnacled to my leg that golden autumnal morning, she maintained a focus that was entirely territorial. "Baby brothers can have my blue bear but they can't have my jaguar." She humphed importantly as she squeezed me tighter, perhaps an instinctive act of protecting her stuffed-animal real estate. Yawning, I rubbed my back absent-mindedly, rolling my empty but still warm mug comfortingly across my sciatica.

When I had gone into the clinic the day before, the doctor had finally recommended that I be induced. My false contractions had been getting stronger but not going anywhere, and I was slowly becoming exhausted. I didn't want to repeat my preparatory experience from my daughter's birth, where I had gone "natural" (they make it sound like a bikini wax) but had tapped all my energy stores long before the really tough labor had even begun.

"You'll get a phone call," the nurse at the desk informed me when I signed out of my appointment.

"When?" I asked, excitedly.

"Sometime tomorrow. Or the next day. Of course, if anything happens 'naturally' before then, go straight to the hospital. But otherwise, because yours is not an actual emergency, your inducement will happen when there's availability in the schedule."

"So I don't even get a window of when the hospital might call?" I asked. "You know, like when you are expecting a repairman?"

"Nope. Sorry." The nurse shrugged. "You'll just have to wait."

"But what if I miss the call?"

"Don't," she said.

A few hours later, the phone rang. Kent and I looked at each other. It rang again. Time froze in our diffusion of responsibility. But it was not the hospital. Nor were the other, oh, like fifty calls that day.

Normally, almost no one calls our home line during the day. Friends use our cells; with a time difference separating us from family, calls to and from loved ones usually happen in the evening. But of course *this* day there were what seemed like endless calls from just about everyone except the hospital. Wrong numbers. Telemarketers. Surveys. The next-door neighbor with a request that her son not be barred from playing the drums even though their soundproofing plans hadn't jelled yet and his drum set was just outside our nursery. My mom. Kent's mom. The grandmas were the worst— they must have called at least three times each. Nothing's worse than a grandma pacing back and forth, chomping at the bit, when new baby meat is about to be dropped into the family zoo cage. These calls came interspersed with automated prescription and appointment reminders. Human resources still fumbling through how to process my maternity-leave paperwork. The doctor's office calling to see whether the hospital had called us yet.

Then, as we were nearing dinner, sometime between *Sesame Street* and when the endless array of crafts had lost their luster, the phone rang.

"Mrs. Weber?" a voice gently asked.

"Yes?" I asked back.

The voice paused—then I could feel the smile spreading in its tone.

"Are you ready to meet your boys?"

And so the day I was sliced open started out like any other day. Although autumn usually meant the beginning of a heavy rain season in the Pacific Northwest, clear morning sunlight danced on the wind-swept water of the canal behind my home. Varsity rowing teams in training were shouldering their way along it, water splitting like shards of glass under their oars. In the distance, the old lift bridge parted the stream of rush-hour traffic, allowing a lone sailboat that had been bobbing patiently to reach the quiet lake beyond.

Carefully, I maneuvered my massive weight down the long staircase of our Victorian home. No easy feat since I literally could not see my feet. Rounding the corner, again quite literally, I braced for the final awkward step into the partially renovated kitchen. Both the kitchen and I embodied an act of expectation and, we also hoped, investment responsibility.

Shuffling around the bright room in my comfy worn-in slippers and maternity robe, I pressed the start button on the coffee maker, making certain to brew decaf. Amidst the odd pieces of lumber and random pipes still strewn about, I managed to find the sugar, not the artificial sweetener. Then I prewarmed the whole milk in my favorite mug, the one I saved for luxurious mornings.

The twins in my belly jostled and rolled like puppies wrestling in a sack. I opened my robe and placed my hand on the thinner material of my nightgown. My palm surfed the wild tumbling just beneath my skin, and I marveled at all that unwilled movement. A little elbow pointing here, a foot extended there. My stomach had never seemed so variedly geometrical. Standing there trying to sip my coffee without lurching forward like a sailor manning some inward-bound ship, I felt like a human popcorn machine.

A figure caught the corner of my eye. I turned to see Kent, my husband, almost arm's reach outside the kitchen window, teetering on the shed rooftop just below and to the right of the deck. Appropriately, he wore his Indiana Jones–type hat as he tossed down debris into the backyard with his usual disregard for danger. I didn't dare yell and startle him. So I leaned my forehead into the cool glass of the window and watched him, an uxorial voyeur, for a while.

This house had taken all we had: all our savings and then some; all our elbow grease, and then some, too. Although it had been "re-muddled" by a string of previous owners, much of its original charm remained intact, and it boasted an extraordinary mountain, water, and city view. Queasy enough with morning sickness, let alone at the prospect of investment in such a project, I had eventually been coaxed by just this breathtaking view into signing the papers despite the wildly overgrown bamboo, the leaky ceilings, the loft full of trash and the hideous textured wallpaper—despite the neighborhood children's voting it the house best suited to host the annual Halloween party, no further decorations required.

Kent looked up and caught me staring at him from the window. He grinned his big, sweet, slightly lopsided grin. The one I fell in love with while far from home. The one that made me feel at home regardless of where we lived.

I smiled back but then added an eye roll at his dangerous renovation antics. I shrugged my shoulders at him in a silent scolding. He merely grinned wider. So I held up my mug and mouthed "Coffee?" He nodded, still smiling, and started his way down the ladder.

Mama don't let your sons grow up to be cowboys . . . I sang under my breath. Or house renovators . . . or real estate investors, I couldn't help but add.

Unobtrusively, something soft and warm had entwined itself with my leg. Instinctively, my hand dropped to rest on the tangled mop of bed-head hair just above my knee. My fingers nestled into the golden curls. A little cheek rested against me and I heard a sleepy sigh. Sweet, spindly arms clad in mermaid princess pajamas pulled my leg closer.

"Will baby brothers *ever* be here?" Our two-and-a-half-year-old daughter, Victoria, looked up at me, whining in all earnestness.

In accordance with the endless stream of doctors and nurses and sonogrammists, we referred to the babies jostling within me as Twin A and Twin B, but after becoming immersed in Dr. Seuss books recently, Victoria preferred calling them Thing 1 and Thing 2. Quite a large Thing 1 and Thing 2, I might add. According to the most recent ultrasound weight estimates, my boys were apparently approaching seven, maybe even eight pounds each. Thing 1 spun around constantly in his womb room but finally settled heavily into the vertex or head-down position, so that for the last few weeks it had felt as if he might be ready to shoot out like a cannon at any moment. Thing 2 stretched transverse, or sideways, across my middle. There he chilled, pretty happily it seemed. His head sat under one of my arms, his feet below the other, wrapped around my rib cage like a love enchilada—with the exception of the occasional sharp kick to keep Mom on her toes.

When the news of twins on the way was first confirmed, my family health practitioners, after a hushed conversation in the hallway, reentered the examination room to inform me that they were referring my prenatal care to a perinatal clinic, a medical team specializing in high-risk pregnancies. I sat there in my tissue-paper robe, taken aback. As someone who associated a high ability to function physically with personal capability and control, I felt uncomfortable at the suggestion of having to be monitored so closely— at being so, well, *fussed over.* The high-risk maternity clinic sat atop a very high tower, a perinatal pinnacle, so to speak: the kind of tower where the elevator takes several minutes to reach the top. It all looked very smart. So much so that I began to feel quite important while rising to the top encased in such elegance.

As the morning sickness of the first trimester subsided, I had been filled with the bizarrely energetic spirit of the second trimester. The hormonal rush that makes you think you can take on the world. The kind and yet cruel trick of nature that lets you race around getting prepared like Wonder Woman on speed for the span of a few weeks, and then dashes you like a bug on a windshield once the exhaustion of the final trimester, birth, nursing (and then pretty much the next twenty years) kicks in. Rising to the top in my second-trimester glory, I reveled in the irrational and yet intoxicating exhilaration of having somehow ended up *doubly* pregnant. I felt as Rebecca must have felt when she felt Esau and Jacob wrestle in her womb. *Hey everyone, I have two in here! TWO!* A real high for an irritating overachiever.

But my pride was short lived. At my first appointment, the staff stamped my medical file with three initials in bold, red ink: AMA. The sound of stamp thudding on paper sounded like the cavernous blow of doom on the door in *Macbeth*.

"AMA? What does that mean?" I ventured to the nurse.

"Advanced maternal age," she smiled at me, compassionately.

"Oh," I tried to smile back. Then I thought about how smiling causes wrinkles.

"You're over age thirty-five," she began to explain. "And then there is . . ." but her words were lost as my eyes fixated on the glowing insignia branded on the manila folder. The damage had been done. My scarlet letters sat hissing on my medical persona, unapologetically.

I'm an old mom, I sighed with them.

No, I'm about to be the old mom of three children under three.

Then it occurred to me, I'm not only going to get older, but now I'm going to get older much, much faster.

"Time for your weekly urine test," the nurse interrupted my

thoughts. "There's a bathroom straight down the hall. Here." She handed me a little container. "Make sure you write your name on the label."

I hesitated. Had my life come to this? The thought of at least thirty-five repeats of this ritual spread out before me.

For the rest of my full-term pregnancy, other than a bad bout with the flu and the increasing difficulty in sliding through tight spaces, my body was strong and the pregnancy even enjoyable. Physically, too, it was easy to forget how good I had it. Warriorlike, I stood ready for birth. Ready, single-handedly, to defeat the Great Curse. The bittersweet blessing of birth that had blessed and blighted women since Eve slept with the serpent and sold out her God-given womanhood for the mere trifling of a vain lie.

Brazenly self-sufficient, I took my supplements. I avoided caffeine and chemicals. I didn't have time to practice yoga, but I did drink all the water I could stomach and tried to breathe deeply a few times a day. I put my feet up when I graded papers. But secretively, to be honest, I harbored a certain pride at how well my pregnancy was going, at how I could "manage it all." The power bar I kept stashed in my disciple's pocket was branded *Performance Pride.* That had long been my mantra, a main tenet of my identity, a golden calf that would have to be pried out of my cold, dead hands.

Which is, pretty much, just about what happened.

1

Four in the Furnace

Imagine a story that puts wood in the fireplace.

SHERMAN ALEXIE

The machine next to me in the hospital room wheezed in and out. I swear it sounded like some dark satanic mill calling my name in rhythmic rasping. "Caro" sucked in, "lyn" droned out.

It was driving me crazy. Ironically, exhausted as I was, I couldn't fall asleep. It's a funny thing, when your own name won't let you rest—a sort of solipsistic insomnia.

Through a narrow slit in the window shade, I watched the light drain out of the day. Slightly elevated against pillows on my hospital bed, I shifted restlessly. Only a short time ago, though it felt like another age by now, we had been admitted to the local hospital and I had signed the consent form to get induced. My fast had begun. Snacking on ice chips only, I then signed the procedure and waiver forms regarding the possibility of my death. No one reads the small print on such things. I was way too excited to concentrate for long, anyway.

The obstetrician on call performed an amniotomy, breaking my first bag of water to induce labor. Usually the instigation of labor with the one twin causes the second to follow suit. But nothing happened for either one. We were instructed to wait. So we waited. And waited. And waited. Kent and I talked. Kent went to get a snack. I read magazines. We made phone calls, being sure to throw a few bones to the grandmothers pawing at the baby news ground. A dear family friend was sitting with Victoria back home; Kent's parents had started their drive up from Portland and would arrive shortly to stay at our house and take over her care. At this point, Victoria was far more excited at the promise of Grandma and Papa coming than about the advent of baby brothers.

I tried putting a pillow over my ears, not easy in my wired position, but the asthmatic machine relentlessly puffed on:

Caro...*lyn*   Caro...*lyn*   Caro...*lyn*   Caro...*lyn*

I looked over at Kent. His large six-foot-five frame hunched contorted into the window seat. I noticed his lips were slightly parted and his brow furrowed—not a peaceful sleep, but a serious, focused one. He started snoring—of course, in a beat completely opposite to the machine so disturbing my peace:

Caro SNORE *lyn*   **Caro** WHISTLE *lyn*   **Caro** SNORE *lyn*   **Caro** WHISTLE *lyn*

The nurse, of course, was again nowhere to be found. I was now also entirely confined to the bed. Helpless, I lay there hooked up to an IV, a catheter, a fetal monitor, a blood-pressure band, my own heart monitor and a contraction screen. I had more wires and tubes and bands surrounding me and attached to me than Frankenstein's monster.

Thus pinned, a very swollen and sleepless butterfly, to a wheel of unknown fortune, I stared at the ceiling in the dim room. And waited. A splinter of light cut across my bed, growing to cover me as the door opened wider. The nurse returned. She checked my vitals and the progress of the twins. We spoke in whispers so as not to disturb Kent, the sight of whose continued contortion made me wince. *How can he sleep like that?* I marveled. However, if there was anything that parenting had taught us recently, it was that sleep was far more important than food or even drink. I respected my husband's acrobatic adherence to this fact. Virginia Woolf should have argued that a woman needs not only a room and money of her own to think and create, but also a good night's sleep. And a long, hot, undisturbed shower without anyone else coming in to use the potty. Or a bubble bath without being stabbed in the back by submerged Barbies.

The nurse looked displeased. There had been very little progress. She must have sensed my unspoken nervousness, because she patted my hand. "Just a minute," she said and returned with the doctor who had broken my water.

"We are going to increase the pitocin dose," he said after examining me. He then explained how this synthetic form of the naturally occurring hormone oxytocin would be introduced into my IV drip so as to jump-start contractions and then help manage the labor. "You should be feeling some action here soon."

Sure enough, a short while later, my contractions began. Soon they were in earnest. I had forgotten how much they could hurt. But I welcomed the familiarity of the feeling, and the fact that it had started at all.

"I think it's time for the epidural," the doctor suggested after his next examination. I understood that this would be necessary. With a planned vaginal birth of multiples, the hospital mandated at least a light epidural in case a medical procedure needed to be done quickly.

That is also why, regardless of how well labor is progressing, all births of multiples, vaginal or caesarean, ultimately take place in the operating room.

I agreed to all these procedures. They seemed commonsense precautions to me, and personally I had nothing to prove otherwise. But secretly I doubted their necessity. I felt confident, clearheaded, so much calmer this second time around.

The nurses were all very kind, the doctor on call jovial. He and my husband hit it off immediately, sharing jokes about their both being pastors' sons. Having been married to the son of a preacher man for some time now, I had come to learn that PKs, or pastors' kids, spoke a language entirely of their own. Something like Klingon.

My regular specialist—"Dr. G" as we referred to him fondly— would be coming in later during labor. The very first thing Kent had noticed about him at our introductory meeting several months earlier was Dr. G's physical strength. "Wow! He has arms like Popeye!" Kent noted with sincere male admiration after Dr. G had left the examination room.

"All the more powerful to extract babies under duress with!" winked the nurse, before adding with all seriousness, "He has the steadiest hands in surgery."

"That's the guy you want in an emergency," Kent nodded seriously.

I hadn't paid much attention. I had decided, *willed*, that there wouldn't be any emergencies.

Normally, whoever is on rotation is the doctor who delivers your baby at most large urban hospitals. But when I asked Dr. G if he could be present, even though he was not on call, he promised to be there. Eventually Twin A had progressed enough that the nurse contacted the doctor. My epidural had begun wearing off at this point, but there was no need (or so I thought) to renew it, as the pain was still relatively dulled but I wanted to have enough feeling to be able to effectively push.

As the doors to the operating room swung open to admit us, we were bathed in ultra-bright light. It felt as if we had entered stage right into a willing suspension of disbelief. The temperature was very cold: a condition of operating rooms so as to help maintain blood pressure. But it didn't register much after the first shiver. As our spotlit gurney plowed through the fourth wall, rather, I felt the adrenaline hit. *Okay, boys,* I thought. *Show time! Or, as Daddy would have it, Game time!* We were all in high spirits, cracking Monty Python jokes about being in an operating room with expensive machines that go "ping!" and laughing about all the "double the trouble" shenanigans we'd surely be in for with twin boys.

Kent was beside himself with joy and anticipation, affirming me and trying to figure out whether the boys should do the same or separate sports. I, too, felt strong and happy. How could I not? It's pretty contagious when the cheerleader of the universe is sitting right next to your ear.

My medical entourage remained small, with only an additional nurse or two joining us once they wheeled me in. The PK doctor on call stood amused at how insistently my first-to-be-born son was stomping on the accelerator to emerge. In vain I tried to slow him down so that our regular doctor could make it in time. Someone called out that he was on his way, fighting traffic. Although it was late at night now, the crowds were just dispersing from a downtown game, so the interstate nearby was bumper to bumper.

"This boy won't wait!" the doctor on call cried out with glee. "And, wow, he's a force!"

We were all laughing while I pushed, or rather, barely assisted, the first twin out into the world. It was more like I was along for his ride.

Look, Ma, no hands! I heard him exclaim joyously in my mind. I somehow managed to stave him off to buy just enough time for Dr. G to sweep into the operating room like an elegant ballroom dancer. Giving us a nod, he bowed low just in time to catch our firstborn son, who bounced, like a basketball, straight out of me.

He's been bouncing, literally, ever since.

"Ooowee, he *is* a strong one!" one of the nurses remarked. *If his strength matches his distinct bloodcurdling cry,* I thought, *he sure must be.* To this day my firstborn son still has a cry that curls paper off the walls.

"Well, if his brother moves the same way, this is going to be a cinch!" The other nurse snapped her fingers and then patted me on the arm.

"What's his name?" she asked.

"Byron Matthew Weber," I replied, exchanging a look of pride and agreement with Kent. "For Kent's grandfather and the poet I was studying when we met; for my brother and Kent's dad's favorite Gospel; and, given his initials, Kent finally gets the BMW he's always wanted!"

The doctor chuckled and Byron stopped crying. Now he studied everything quietly with big bright eyes. The nurses fussed all over him—he particularly charmed the gals right away. Another Byronic trait I somehow suspected I'd need to watch closely.

Smirking at this obvious bundle of fun, I turned my focus to my second, yet unborn son. While I ached to cuddle Byron, I knew that I had to concentrate, that we weren't all in the clear yet.

Dr. G's eyes smiled at me over his mask. "All right, Caro," he said, "you know what to do!"

I started pushing. I felt the second twin start to turn inside me. *Hooray! Here we go!* I inwardly rejoiced, and pushed again.

Nothing.

I waited, caught my breath, pushed again.

Nothing.

I waited for the crescendo on my next contraction. I didn't realize that I shouldn't be feeling the contractions at all within my body but only be alert to them on the screen. Feeling them meant my epidural had waned considerably. But I followed the nurse's prompts without questioning. I had never experienced a full epidural before: compared to my natural first birth with a doula, and then riding now on the joy from the safe and quick arrival of my first twin, this version felt, well, easier (if that's even a word one can use with good conscience in describing any kind of birth).

But something didn't feel quite right.

"Push harder, love," one of the nurses encouraged in a British accent. She leaned against me to help hold me up higher, so I could angle my strength better.

"I *am* . . ." I gritted my teeth. I was working really hard now. Panic fluttered inside me like a caged bird.

Nothing.

"Rest for a minute, dear." The other nurse came to my side.

I leaned back, trying to catch my breath.

"Call in more staff!" Dr. G demanded of the head nurse. "And get the other doctor back in here, too. Right now."

"There's an emergency next door," she answered him. "Another mother went into high-risk labor."

Kent and I looked at each other with *what are the chances?* written on our faces.

"It's not good," I heard her add, quietly, to a nearby intern. I wasn't sure to whom she was referring, me or the other mother. It didn't matter. We were one and the same. Through the walls, I felt the other patient's fear. Utterly helpless, I did all I could do: I thought a prayer for her and then one for me. *Hang in there,* I telepathed to her, squeezing my eyes shut as though to ensure the delivery of the message. *We're in this together.*

When I opened them, I immediately noticed what I could only describe as a shapeless darkness looming in the far corner, opposite to where Kent was sitting next to me—connecting me, perhaps, to this other woman in labor? But how could we be connected by a shapeless darkness? That didn't seem to make any sense. I instinctively shook my head, trying to clear my thoughts and my vision. But the darkness remained, formless but distinct.

As the next contraction swelled, I began pushing again. This baby felt slower. Then something stopped. I tried and tried but couldn't seem to push him any further. I looked at the clock. It had only been a few minutes, but it felt like an eternity since my first son had been born. A nurse brought him, cleaned and swaddled now, toward me so I could see him. But just as I turned my head, Dr. G urged me to push.

I tried, but nothing happened. It felt like I was pushing against a wall. The nurse set Byron on my chest, partly so I could admire him and partly to encourage me. He was beautiful, of course. But he seemed to be looking at me quizzically, as though in search of his in utero döppelganger.

"It's no use," Dr. G announced.

"Give me another chance," I begged.

"We don't have much time, Carolyn. I can try to manually move him." I nodded.

Quickly, he tried to turn the baby around. Twin B was lying sideways, but he was supposed to have moved head down into the vacuum created by his brother's exit. And indeed he had started to, hence the initial movement I had felt. But then he had lodged. This became apparent after several unsuccessful attempts at pushing him further down the birth canal. Dr. G was now trying to manually turn the baby around to assist him in coming out. I tried pushing again, with Dr. G guiding the baby from inside.

Still, nothing.

Suddenly I felt a sharp pain. I sucked my breath in as Dr. G pulled himself up. We locked eyes.

Kent squeezed my hand. "What is it?" he asked nervously.

"The baby is stuck." Dr. G rubbed his forehead with his upper arm since his gloves were bloody.

"What do you mean he's stuck?" Kent asked.

"Well, he hasn't turned head down all the way. His hands are beside his head, and his head is big enough to begin with." Dr. G nodded at Kent's own big head (a Weber trait, oh lucky me). I rolled my eyes, in spite of the anxiety.

"Sometimes the vacuum created by the first twin's birth creates a helpful suction, aiding the second twin's position, but sometimes it hinders things. In this case, it's hindering. He's been pulled down in a Y shape. There's no way to push him out, at least not without too much risk to both of you. We are going to have to get him out surgically."

"No . . ." I started. "I can do this . . ." I sat up and tried pushing again, but it was no use. I slumped back, exhausted. Defeated. I gave Kent a frightened look.

"We don't have the time to keep trying," Dr. G explained quickly. "He's getting limited oxygen, and soon his blood pressure will be dropping more quickly. As is yours." He added gently, "Caro . . ."

We locked eyes again. All the joking had now stopped. The room was dead still. Even my first son had ceased fussing. I looked over at him, a little blue mound resting in the glass bassinette by the scales.

"It's time," Dr. G said to the handful of us, waiting.

And then he shouted a single word that slivered the antiseptic stillness.

"CONVERT!"

A sudden tsunami of frantic energy rose up as the operating room swelled around me. I grabbed onto Kent with my eyes. The scene instantaneously transformed from a small group of laughing intimates to a highly synchronized frenzy of countless nurses and interns, focused now. And quiet.

Things grew serious. Fast.

Dr. G's voice rose again, steady and determined. "We'll need to operate," he called out over his medical hive. He leaned over and explained, very quickly, that I would have to be restrained and that it was immeasurably important that I lie very, very still, though that shouldn't be a problem, given my epidural earlier. Or so we both thought.

"Although it's an extreme measure, we can put you entirely under," Dr. G called out.

"No, no," I insisted. "I will be okay."

I didn't want to miss the arrival of my second son. I didn't want to come to without any memory of anything. I wanted to see his face as I had seen his siblings'. And, if I was completely honest, I also didn't want to lose control, or at least the semblance of it. Losing control is not one of my gifts.

In the rush of bodies swirling around me, one face came forward, appearing directly in front of mine. It introduced itself as my anesthesiologist. The face was startlingly white, with clear blue eyes. I found myself wondering if he was an albino.

"We do not have time to renew your epidural, Carolyn," the anesthesiologist spoke quickly. "We'd need to turn you over and reinsert another dose into your spine. But we can't move you now. Not at all."

I steadied myself for deep waters.

"I am giving you something in your IV that should help immediately, however, just to be sure." He patted my arm.

Everything was moving very fast and very slow, all at the same time. A strange, surreal present.

An intense gloom seeped into my peripheral vision. Certain that the darkness that kept lurking in the corner would dissipate once under scrutiny, I fixed my eyes on it. It didn't fade away. In fact, it looked bigger, darker, more threatening somehow. Such a darkness defied reason, given the bright lights of the operating room. And yet there it was. So intangibly tangible that it felt more like a personification than an inference. The machine that had been chanting my name began slowing down its pronunciation. The effect was like a record being played on the wrong speed. I couldn't help but think the rendition made a mockery of whatever song my life might have been.

By now I was strapped down, crucifixlike, to the gurney. Only my head could move, just a little, to turn left toward Kent's face, straight forward toward the anesthesiologist's, or right, past the machines and IV drip, toward the simmering darkness in an otherwise gaudily lit room. As I was draped with a curtain and prepped for the emergency caesarean delivery of my second son, the anesthesiologist never moved from my direct line of vision. Without once wavering, he spoke reassuringly and kindly. He included Kent, too, in his explanations; his face, however, remained directly above mine.

Without warning, I felt the incision. The blade traveled from left to right across my lower abdomen, in what I can only describe as a searing white-hot pain that took my breath away.

"Stop!" I finally managed to get out. My tongue felt fuzzy. My words emerged garbled. I couldn't move my limbs much, either, and yet I could feel the surgery taking place. Everything seemed beyond my control. One look at my face and Kent knew in an instant. He shrank back, horrified.

"Wait!" he shouted for me.

The medical team froze and looked at him.

"I could feel the cut!" I told them.

The doctor gave me a look of disbelief.

"I felt the cut—it just went from your right to left!" I repeated.

Silence.

This is what it must have been like to be drawn and quartered. I distinctly remember recalling the saints.

"She's not responding in time to the medication," a nurse offered.

"For some people there is a delay, it's rare, but it can happen. Look, I can't up it anymore," the anesthesiologist shouted over his shoulder. "The kidneys . . . the baby . . . She'll need something else."

"She needs to go under," Dr. G stated authoritatively.

Panicked, I glanced at the clock. Fifteen minutes since my first son had been born. A lifetime—or a death time—in a twin birth.

Under the clock, I noticed that the strange shadow in the corner of the room had grown even larger. Like a Prufrockian fog, it approached my cot, curling its fingers and tail around my feet and hands. Unable to move, I inwardly recoiled. Yet no one else seemed aware of it. The medical team kept moving around it, through it. Kent kept looking right at me, sending me his strength through his eyes.

A wave of fear washed over me, followed quickly by grief and despair. But then reality hit me, too. Maybe going under full anesthesia would be best? To simply sink into nothingness? What to do? *What to do?*

All this time, the anesthesiologist's face remained intimately above mine. I will see that face before me for as long as I live, and somehow, I suspect, when I cease to live. Here, at least. "Caro." His astonishingly blue eyes pierced my soul. "Listen." I couldn't put my finger on the look he wore. It wasn't anxious, or worried, or even frightened. Perhaps I could only best describe it as concerned. And strangely, somehow, utterly trustworthy. And, well, *loving*. I should have done anything but listened, let alone heeded. I should have screamed, or taken the perinatalist's command. Perhaps I should have fainted, or fought.

But I didn't.

Instead, I remained very, very still. My thoughts steadied first and foremost, with complete clarity, on my unborn son. I listened carefully as the anesthesiologist spoke quickly, quietly and yet very clearly.

"I don't think you should go under." His words traveled through his mask. "There are serious risks—especially in your situation. Not only can you aspirate your vomit, but . . ."

"Let's go!" yelled Dr. G.

The anesthesiologist looked over at the doctor, then back at me. "Your son is already under incredible duress," the anesthesiologist whispered furiously. "There isn't time to manage the pain, at least not without major consequences for either one or both of you."

I nodded that I understood. It was becoming increasingly difficult, for some reason, to form words.

"You can do this, but you'll need to remain perfectly still. Do you understand? *Perfectly still.*"

Kent quietly started praying next to me. He squeezed my hand tighter, as though sending all of his strength through to me.

"Carolyn, here." The anesthesiologist took my one hand; Kent had a firm grip on the other. "I can get you through this. Please, trust me."

The room flashed dark. Was I blacking out? Or had the shadow in the room now overcome it entirely? I couldn't tell where consciousness ended and dreaming began.

"Her blood pressure is dropping fast," I heard a woman's voice say from far, far away.

For a moment I could taste terror in my mouth, a tinny fear that toppled all my dreams and fastened me, like the medical cords, helpless to my little cot of existence. Amidst all the busyness around me melting away into the mounting dark, I felt forsaken, forgotten.

Lost.

I sighed, unsure which way to drift.

A thought fuzzily surfaced. Inwardly my unborn son came into focus again, his unmet face bobbing before me like a beacon. I knew that getting him out alive, and hopefully without additional complications, overruled everything. I knew that my life was his. His, mine. Even more so. And then the other thoughts rolled through my desert like tumbleweed: My firstborn son, blinking in his bassinette, waiting for his brother. My daughter's face as I left for the hospital—it seemed so long ago now but had only been earlier that day: her trepidation at my going but measured excitement at the promise of new brothers. Her little hand waving from the window, her small body plastered against the glass in her homemade "I'm the big sister!" T-shirt. My sister's excited voice on the phone. Grandparents high on joy. Kent. My Kent. And years of loving and being loved . . .

Everything whittled down into a tiny point of light.

The whole world inblooms, a rose folding back onto itself: now only a bud remaining, enwrapping my husband, my son, and me amidst the thorns.

And yet someone else is *there.*

Suddenly, that tiny point of diamond-bright light pierced my eyes, parting the darkness, loosening its grip on my limbs, alleviating its heaviness. The obscurity scurried back to its corner, reduced somehow, while the beam of light widened to illuminate the anesthesiologist's face above me. For a moment, he appeared haloed.

I look straight into the light and my eyes are pierced to the clear by the unspeakable beauty of the remembrance: God chose to love us through death, into life. Love, the only thing worth living, and dying, for. Love, the only thing for which there is no regret, and for which nothing is wasted.

So in the end, as it must always come to be when faith reaches the end of the sidewalk, there really was no decision. Only acquiescence. Only at-one-ment. The breath moved through me and from me into the only way of being that really matters.

"Carolyn?" The anesthesiologist's kind voice felt achingly familiar. "Are you ready?"

"Yes," I said, looking straight into those deep cerulean eyes.

They smiled back at me over the medical mask. Blue as the sea on the wing of a dove.

And then, a great peace descended on me.

The book of Daniel tells us that the mighty King Nebuchadnezzar made a massive image of gold. Then he decreed that all the nations and peoples of every language, at the sound of the music, must fall down and worship this idol. Whoever refused was to be immediately thrown into a blazing furnace. Therefore, as soon as they heard the music, all the nations and peoples of every language fell down and worshiped the image of gold that King Nebuchadnezzar had set

up. But then it came to King Nebuchadnezzar's attention that three
Jews named Shadrach, Meshach and Abednego refused to serve his
gods or worship the image of gold. Furious with rage, Nebuchadnezzar summoned these men, warning them that if they did not fall
down and worship the image he made, they would be thrown immediately into a blazing furnace. "Then," he said, "what god will be
able to rescue you from my hand?"

Shadrach, Meshach and Abednego replied, "King Nebuchadnezzar, we do not need to defend ourselves before you in this matter.
If we are thrown into the blazing furnace, the God we serve is able
to deliver us from it, and he will deliver us from Your Majesty's
hand. But even if he does not, we want you to know, Your Majesty,
that we will not serve your gods or worship the image of gold you
have set up."

Furious with Shadrach, Meshach and Abednego, Nebuchadnezzar ordered the furnace heated seven times hotter than usual and
commanded some of the strongest soldiers in his army to tie up the
three men and throw them into the blazing furnace. The flames had
grown so hot that their heat killed the soldiers who stood nearby.

Then King Nebuchadnezzar leaped to his feet in amazement and
asked his advisers, "Weren't there three men that we tied up and
threw into the fire?"

They replied, "Certainly, Your Majesty."

The king cried, "Look! I see four men walking around in the fire,
unbound and unharmed, and the fourth looks like a son of the gods."

Then Nebuchadnezzar approached the opening of the blazing
furnace and shouted, "Shadrach, Meshach and Abednego, servants
of the Most High God, come out! Come here!"

And so the story ends: "Shadrach, Meshach and Abednego came
out of the fire, and the satraps, prefects, governors and royal advisers

crowded around them. They saw that the fire had not harmed their bodies, nor was a hair of their heads singed; their robes were not scorched, and there was no smell of fire on them" (Dan 3:1-30).

Time pours out like water, covering my body. I do not drown, but rather float.

I can't see my babies. It takes all I have to move myself beyond the pain. Some nurses mistake my silence for comfort. They don't realize that I can bear anything silently. Practice makes perfect.

Though this perfect is a different kind of practice.

Under the constant gaze of the anesthesiologist, my husband and I hold each other in our eyes, as we did during our wedding vows. An oath, for better or for worse. In sickness and in health. They should add "in crisis and in emergency, in pain and in silence." A vow, especially before God, means having given your word speaks for you even when you can no longer speak.

Kent remains calm, present, giving me as always what I need. I feel us growing closer in those brief moments than most lovers do in a lifetime. I need to get this baby out safely. He knows this and sustains me.

I hang suspended, my body perfectly still. I hold on to the pain, saying nothing, as though I were holding my breath. I wince under the tugging and pulling. I am told it won't be much longer. But it is. Long. For me.

Despite how we like to think our time in this fallen dimension, *chronos*, measures quantity so precisely, it is God's perfect time, or *kairos*, that is always about quality. How time shifts speeds and yet remains the same in measurement seems to attest to the underlying reality of *kairos* to *chronos*.

And then . . .

An infant cry! A joyful noise! A new song!

"William Stuart Weber," Kent announces, almost sobbing. This second son, named for Kent's beloved father, for a string of beloved fathers before him. He arrives in our world calm; he doesn't cry loudly or for long. He gives me a pensive look when they hold him up for me to see. He, too, suspended in time—lifted in a quality that cannot be measured, in *kairos*—studies me, and I him. He opens his arms wide, as if to embrace me. The Moro reflex: I ground myself in the scientific. Except that his newborn face betrays no fear, no startling: only serenity, a surveying certitude. His entire body bursts forth as a radiant Blakean declaration: "I'm here!"

I begin to feel loopy, not certain if it's from relief or joy or the medication finally kicking in. I can still feel the stitches taking place, though each one grows fainter in its infliction. I search the room, but any trace of the darkness is gone. Studying my son, I feel a deep peace. Even—dare I say it?—the *Holy*.

I start shaking, hard. I can't stop it or control it. The nurses wrap me in warm blankets. I sit, like my sons, cocooned and blinking.

"Belated drug high." Dr. G removes his gloves and mask and pats my knee. "And a hormonal drop."

"And shock," the young female intern adds, touching my arm.

"It's to be expected," Dr. G says matter-of-factly. As usual, he is professionalism personified. But then he gently moves the hair from my cheek before he prepares to leave. I notice that his brow is drenched in sweat. A drop falls on my cheek.

"You have one amazing lady there, son." The anesthesiologist's eyes dance over his mask at Kent. "You have both run a good race. Together." Then he gives me a look I will never forget. Of endearment? Of gentle pride? Of cherishing? Again, I couldn't quite say. So much about him inexpressible! But a look that holds my look, and that replies in return: all is well, all is good.

A look that smiles, "See?"

Later, he came to my hospital room to check up on me. An unrequired visit: anesthesiologists do not usually follow up with their patients. Gently, he sat and held my hand as he explained to me what happened, why the first drugs had failed and the interaction of events that followed. He told me of the other multiple births he had witnessed, of the mother who went under but never emerged. Of the loss of one of the babies. Of the reasons for his coaching.

He came in a haze; I do not know if I dreamt him or not. By then I was heavily sedated, finally sinking into sleep after the adrenaline crash. No—I did not dream him. But I could not say he seemed completely of this world, either.

At the time in that dim hospital room, I was too exhausted to do much more than listen. But listening, *real listening*, I have come to learn, is one of the great gifts of exhaustion, of trauma. All I can say with utmost certainty is his presence made me glad. A wave of sleep carried me off, and when I woke he was gone. In the rush of recovery, and the nursing and packing up and taking home of new twins, I never did get his name.

But in my story I like to think it was Emmanuel.

2

The Widow's Offering

*Pour out your heart like water
in the presence of the Lord.*

LAMENTATIONS 2:19

I couldn't afford therapy, so I started writing.

Not the academic pieces I had done for so long in my profession, but the soul-pouring, self-introspective, even at times extremely painful kind. Following the near-death birth, I wrote my heart out. Writing in bits and pieces throughout the day. Keeping a journal with me like a papery doppelgänger, bound to my every move. Trauma cracks us open (or for some of us, cuts us open) so the Holy Spirit can get in. So we can "right" ourselves.

Whenever I tried to sleep in the months following the birth, I found—for the first time in my life—I couldn't. It would begin in the very act of lying down. Just settling into a horizontal position was enough for my body to snap into memory mode. I would feel again the cut from the emergency surgery. The adrenaline rushed through my body. I would toss and turn on a sea of troubles, fear after fear playing in my mind. Irrational scenarios played out before me like hands dealt by the devil. Worries and anxieties: replays from how the birth *could've* gone to the current threats to my children's safety. A tightness in my chest that my husband could be taken easily from me at any moment, as could any of the children, or other loved ones. Or I could be dying, some unknown, unnamed ailment gnawing at me from inside. Or some misstep in judgment, or random act of crime, could rob me of a loved one.

Barely able to stand, quite literally, during the physical recovery of my abdominal muscles, I returned to the classroom, teaching an extra-heavy class load to make up for my unforeseen extended medical leave so that I would still be eligible for my sabbatical. My family doctor recommended postpartum counseling, as did a few close friends. I discovered, however, that counseling could be very expensive, and our health insurance (like most American plans) did not cover the cost. And I remained emotionally hesitant.

Eventually, however, the poor sleep and increased anxiety trumped the fee. Insomnia coupled with the already taxing nighttime schedule of nursing multiples had led to such exhaustion that I grew more sleep deprived than I had ever known. I felt absolutely raw, as though my skin had been stripped off and every nerve was exposed to a bracing wind. My brain was also beginning to shut down—not a handy thing for a professor. And then to my surprise, troubling memories and deep anger as well as despair over unresolved issues from my past began to surface. Though I had always been reticent to seek help, I knew it was time to take some sort of action—if not for me, then for my marriage and my children.

On top of other medical and care costs incurred by my recovery, we managed to scrape together enough to try a few months of post-partum counseling. Fortunately, I found an excellent therapist. Perceptive and empathic, she was also pragmatic and brought years of professional and personal experience to postpartum struggles. She looked leonine, with a great mane of curly blond hair and big green eyes, her beauty only heightened by an air of sincere intelligence. She always wore boots and long, flowing skirts. It was like Stevie Nicks meets Sappho. We discussed my journal entries, and her additional writing exercises proved incredibly helpful.

Shortly after our first session, I had a telling dream. In it, I found myself pinned to a table, much like a butterfly on a wheel. In fact, I physically resembled a butterfly, with wings instead of arms outspread, vulnerable and terrified. A beautiful woman stood over me, carefully extracting the pins while speaking reassuringly to me in a calm, distinct voice. I began to feel peaceful, even hopeful, at being freed. I did not doubt it would happen. She wore a white coat but looked less like a doctor than like an angel.

A character in one of T. S. Eliot's plays announces to a couple obsessed with the Freudian psychoanalysis that was the rage at the time: "You don't need therapy, you need salvation."[1] Similarly, Kathleen Norris observes that "modern believers tend to trust in therapy more than in mystery," a fact she uses to explain the church's tendency to feed its sheep pop-culture psychology and feel-good self-help speech rather than the direct, unmitigated power of the Bible.[2]

I had to admit, when it came to seeking counseling, I trod skeptically at first. In the end, however, I found my experience to be an immensely healing one for which I will remain forever grateful. I began to discover how therapy unraveled some of the mystery and, for me, also reverentially intensified it. As a result, I realized that my "psyche" need not be severed; soul and spirit (that is, my spirit along with that of the Holy Spirit) *can* work together. In fact, they prefer to.

And when they do, glimpses of the mystery of salvation become revealed, and actually enacted.

This therapist played a key role in helping me understand that trauma, while horrific and something we would never wish or pray for, can offer profound personal movement toward the healing of other, deeper wounds. It is like the proverbial intersection of the Chinese symbol for "crisis" and "opportunity": the first morphs into the other.

If there's anything I've come to learn in life, it's that more often than not, emotional pain is far more significant than physical pain. Sure, the latter stinks. It clouds our vision and throws everything into survival relief. When I am focused in childbirth, or miserable with a head cold, or puking in a bucket, I don't feel much like meditating on Scripture. In fact, what often comes to my mind or out of my mouth (to my personal embarrassment and testimony as a sinner) is far from reverent. To me, the fact that Jesus quoted from the Psalms as he hung in excruciating agony is all the more proof of his sinlessness. His death moan intersects the pinnacles of utter and complete physical and emotional anguish, and yet the answer is *still* to cry out to God. Perhaps such a moment is precisely when it is most crucial to do so.

My therapist explained to me how over several years of treating clients, she had witnessed multiple instances of physical trauma's bringing of previous buried emotional trauma to the surface. I began to see the connection, especially as my own demons came out, quite literally in some ways, from my having been cut open.

Even the demons recognize who Jesus is. They are purged by prayer and come out in his name. Therapy, when used as a means of growing closer to Christ, I found, becomes a powerful naming tool. Once fears are "spoken away," they lose their grip over you. As I wrote out and prayed through old wounds, coupled with newly appreciated joys, I began to see how grace indeed makes us a new creation (2 Cor 5:17). I grew further from my demons and closer to God. The nightmares ceased, and sleep (though still short) came deeper and peacefully. I began to see how even the most gaping of holes can be sutured closed so healing can begin. And that we are more precious for the scar.

❋

I love how the Bible gives us templates for real-life living. Skeptics like to poke holes in the stories: they often keep up the refrain that the Bible is irrelevant to us today. But I have yet to experience any text that is more relevant to each of us, always and without exception. There is something for everyone, and something for every time, and something for every life season in this Great Book.

The Gospels offer two renditions of a wonderful story in which a poor woman of the most vulnerable rank in her society gives generously in honor of her God. It is the parable of the widow who contributes all of her paltry income to the temple treasury. As I poured out my story for God, exhausted from the simultaneous creative processes of authoring and mothering, I kept returning to this story in my heart's mind.

Here is Luke's version. I always admire Luke's precision and efficiency. His medical training is apparent in his reporting, and the boilerplate is good for me, the often too-loquacious English teacher:

> As Jesus looked up, he saw the rich putting their gifts into the temple treasury. He also saw a poor widow put in two very small copper coins. "Truly I tell you," he said, "this poor widow has put in more than all the others. All these people gave their

gifts out of their wealth; but she out of her poverty put in all she had to live on." (Lk 21:1-4)

Giving God your all rarely has to do with actual money. Looking at the parable of the poor widow who gave her last coins to the offering, I considered what it is to give God everything, to truly give him significant pieces of yourself until you have given him your all. To give so much that all that is left is to *be* with him. I think of how the world measures the depth of our giving by what we hand over, but Jesus measures it by what we hold on to.

As Norris points out, however, "To give up oneself in love, or dedication, one must have a self."[3]

Good point.

So I found myself wondering, how do we attain this self? A self that is even worth giving up?

"Always give yourselves fully to the work of the Lord, because you know that your labor in the Lord is not in vain" (1 Cor 15:58). But what happens when you feel you have nothing left to give? When all you have is an empty bowl? That you are crawling to the finish line, feeling far from having run a glorious race? What does the coin represent then?

I wonder if some direction can be found in discerning different kinds of "poverty"—looking to what "meekness" means in the biblical sense, for instance, as the Beatitudes so beautifully show us. When it comes to considering the dimensions of poverty, widows in particular, I think, become loaded metaphors. We are told again and again to help provide for those less fortunate than ourselves, and widows would certainly fall into this category, especially in biblical times. With rare exceptions, a woman without a man had no physical protection or financial provision. She could not be represented politically or often socially, and she would be utterly dependent on the next of kin.

We see this situation perfectly in the story of Ruth, the young widow for whom the Old Testament book is named. Though she cleaves to her late husband's family and faith, she must provide for herself and glean from the edges of a relative's field. She is at the mercy of her "kinsman redeemer" under the laws of surplice instated by Moses at God's command for the benefit of those less fortunate, the literal marginalized, who would be allowed access to the perimeters of the wealthier for survival.

But what happens when we take the metaphor a step further? In the central image of the bridegroom and the bride as representative of Christ and the church, widowhood takes on even greater spiritual implications. The bride is often represented as adulterous—the woman (God's people) who was loved, cared for, and adorned, but who spurned her lover (God) and preferred the attentions of (or giving attention to) another (other gods, idols, anything that is other than God).

Paradox lies at the center of God's mystery. For in the emptying of ourselves, even in the rendering up of the realization that we may not have a self, we find ourselves filled in and fulfilled by the presence of God. Like the old saying goes, "the heart which gives, receives."

"Coins," then, can be encouraging words, a prayer, simple fellowship, the offer of companionship, empathy, compassion, even mutual support in silence. While spiritual poverty is quicksand, its *recognition* can be a stepping-stone to wealth in God. It can, if we let it, foster the roots of humility, the meekness of the Beatitudes that will be richly compensated in the currency that truly matters.

I found myself nudged into wondering: just what are my "widow's coins"? The academic sabbatical occurs every seventh year. With tenure and my sabbatical on the horizon, and having touched death through birth, what debt had I now to pay?

The Gospel of Mark's version of the same story of the widow's offering includes a few additional telling details that help us answer questions like these.

> Jesus sat down opposite the place where the offerings were put and watched the crowd putting their money in to the temple treasury. Many rich people threw in large amounts. But a poor widow came and put in two very small copper coins, worth only a few cents.
>
> Calling his disciples to him, Jesus said, "I tell you the truth, this poor widow has put more into the treasury than all the others. They all gave out of their wealth; but she, out of her poverty, put in everything—all she had to live on." (Mk 12:41-44)

While the rich people "threw" in their donations, the poor widow "put" in hers. The rich are, quite literally, able to toss their money about without much concern, while the poor are keenly conscious of what they give. The rich givers seem far more nonchalant than the poor woman, who gives with care and places her money in the collection with deliberate gentleness, suggesting reverence. The act is meaningful for her, not only because her sacrifice is proportionately greater but because her love for her God is present in her gift.

Jesus, as Mark skillfully notes, sits "opposite" to the offering receptacle. From this voyeur stance, his observations pass undetected. But he also sits, like the moral of the story he is telling, in opposition to all that "the world" holds about status and wealth. Jesus' very position upholds God's preference for quality over quantity. And it provides insight into how he knows the very secrets of our hearts.

For all God had given me, a great wave of gratitude swept in. As I sat in my usual café, pouring out thoughts in my journal during the few minutes left on the babysitting clock, my mind kept returning to the story of the ten lepers from Luke 17:11-19. Jesus heals all ten lepers, but only one returns to give thanks. And in that giving of thanks, he is *fully* healed.

As I meditated on this story, I realized I could no longer hesitate to give thanks through my own story. I had sought the Lord's mercy, and he had given it to me abundantly. Now I needed to turn back to Jesus, give thanks, receive that fuller healing.

That is the truth of tithing: we give back one-tenth in response to the original gift, and then God completes the rest of the cycle of blessing over again, ad infinitum (quite literally). As fallen beings, marked by the selling out of ourselves at the serpent's hiss, we do put our mouths where our money is: we mark commitment by investment. But "investment" means so much more than the accumulation of monies. Investment is also what builds in us, and ahead of us. It is the worth of the present, and the giving of that present's worth into the future. We appreciate through appreciation.

A few months later, I sucked in my breath as I signed a book contract to write my conversion story, knowing somewhere in my being that I was most likely signing away the other love that up to this point had most vied for God's place: my academic career. I imagined it tinkling like coins when I placed it in the collection plate.

⁂

During the months of drafting those early chapters, I was also beginning to prepare my application for promotion to tenure as an associate professor. It can be a harrowing process with a do-or-die undertone, usually taking six years of careful assessment, with tenure granted or denied by the end of the sixth year. If granted tenure, the professor receives all the security and accolades of a long-term professional establishment. If denied tenure, the professor leaves the institution with a significant blot on his or her record, or at the very least, a difficult impediment to overcome if a career at another university is pursued. So the untenured professor often undergoes fear, uncertainty and much anxiety throughout the process. Some of my colleagues who have received tenure have celebrated the achievement with more relief, relish and panache than one would a marriage or a birth.

When I tried explaining tenure to a friend of mine who works in sales, he laughed. "Wow!" He shook his head. "You mean, you only get evaluated for seven years, and then, if you make it, you're set for life?"

I guess when you put it that way, the drama drains out of it.

Then again, as for anyone in any situation, it is all relative. Thank goodness our God is a God for whom no prayer is too small.

I tried to keep such an objective perspective as I prepared my file, but remaining objective about your hitherto entire life passion can be a bit tricky. My teaching and service areas were strong, and I had contributed to the scholarship in my area of research in the field of romantic studies. What made me nervous, actually, involved revealing my current work on my conversion story, and my growing interest in the intersection of my faith with academia.

So far, I had managed to remain relatively quiet about my faith when it came to campus dynamics. Sure, students and colleagues who were close to me knew of my beliefs, but I had been careful not to explicitly share these in the classroom or scare others with off-putting proselytizing. I refrained from writing "Jesus saves!" in red ink while correcting papers. I had learned this lesson early in the game.

For instance, once during an interview for an academic position, I was asked to put my teaching philosophy into a single sentence. After a moment of reflection, I responded: "To love my students into understanding."

Around the table some people raised their eyebrows, while others set down their pens with an audible huff. A few appeared downright scandalized. Only one or two people gave me a knowing nod. Outwardly, I tried to remain poised in my polished cream interview suit, but inward I reeled: what had I done? Frantic, I looked around the table as I floundered to explain what I meant.

"I hope to move my students into a better understanding of themselves and their world through my passion for teaching and discussion of literature." No one moved or said a thing. I swallowed hard and added, "I want them to experience the love of learning, what really matters in an education, making it all worthwhile." I sensed I was stepping to the edge of a very steep cliff.

An uneasy silence ensued, punctuated by a few coughs.

Finally one senior colleague broke the stillness. She slid her glasses down her nose and then tilted her head down to peer over the frames at me. In look and speech, she personified the direction "down." *That's where I'm headed in this interview,* I remember thinking to myself. *Down.*

"I don't think it appropriate to love students," she said brusquely. By her tone, I understood she was taking "love" in anything but its *agape* form.

I opened my mouth to defend myself yet again, but shut it when I caught the eye of another colleague sitting nearby. The topic was quickly changed by another professor, and the long interrogation began on which theorists were currently my favorites and what courses would I be most qualified to teach.

Later, this well-meaning professor took me aside. "Look, Dr. Weber," he said very kindly, "we certainly want you here. We would be privileged to have you here . . ."

"Thank you," I interrupted him heartily. The institution looked like a wonderful place to be.

"But I must warn you," he said gently, "you cannot go around saying such things as 'loving students into understanding.' It will get you in, well, in *trouble*, you know."

Still academically green, I turned pink.

"Look," he continued, in kind address to my discomfort, "most academics don't get the 'Christ thing.' It makes them, well, ah, *nervous*. A few of your interviewers were really offended by what you said. To the point where, even in spite of what you can bring to the table, I am not sure they will vote for you."

I shuddered, uneasy at having jeopardized my interview. And saddened. I had so enjoyed meeting the students here, teaching a sample class. I had already started loving them into understanding . . . *oooh, stop that,* I scolded myself.

"But why?" I asked, partly to him, partly to myself.

He looked at me but didn't say anything.

"Okay." I backed up. "Even if we remove the love principle, the way I feel God's pleasure when I teach . . ." He smiled, in spite of himself, at that one.

"Isn't that a doctrine going back to Sidney, perhaps at least as old as Horace," I rushed on, "that teaching should delight? That we learn best when we are moved and delighted?"

"Just rephrase," he said, again kindly, but more firmly.

Though disturbed in some strange way I couldn't quite put my finger on, I nodded in agreement.

With such experiences in mind, I now approached a range of colleagues from all over—former professors, contacts from conferences, friends from graduate school, trusted specialists in my field—for their input on whether I should publish a work about my faith while going up for tenure. A handful of those I consulted were believers; most were not. The feeling, for the most part, especially from unbelievers, was united: *Don't.*

Once when I was out of town for a conference, I ran into a former colleague. Since I admired his esteemed record and knew I could trust him, I decided to ask Grant for his objective advice. He graciously invited me to lunch at his faculty lounge. After a helpful conversation about scholarship, teaching and service, this senior colleague began to wrap things up: "Well, Carolyn, all your categories for tenure look strong. I don't think you should have any questions or concerns . . ."

"I do have another project in the works," I finally told him. "But I'm not sure how best to describe it."

"A writing project?" he asked as the waitress cleared our plates.

"Yes."

"Good, oh good. Has it been accepted for publication?" He wiped his mouth with his napkin.

"Yes."

"Even better!" He set his napkin down with a flourish.

I thought of the jaded academic Bernard's ironic pronouncement summing up the golden calf of academia in Tom Stoppard's witty play *Arcadia*: "Publish!"[4]

"Is it creative or scholarly?" he asked, leaning in.

"I guess you could say it's a little bit of both." I shrugged.

"Hmmm. What is it about?" He continued to look over the dessert menu.

Still the furtive Christian amidst what more often than not proved to be enemy territory—the secular university campus—I was grateful not to make eye contact. I took a deep breath.

"My conversion to Christianity," I replied, trying to sound nonchalant, though my pulse raced wildly in my throat. In comparison to this highly accomplished colleague with full professor status, I felt very young and very, well, *untenured*. I sank down further into my chair.

Silence.

Although he had stopped studying his option in sweets, he kept his head bowed. He didn't say anything. The stillness grew so uncomfortable that I ventured into it and made some noise. A bad habit of mine.

"Oh, no, no . . ." he rubbed his eyes with his hands, keeping his head bowed. Then he set the menu down. "No, that won't do . . ."

"What do you mean . . . ?" My voice trailed off.

"I suppose it's all religious, and then you said, 'Christian,' right? That means you'll probably have to go and mention that *Jesus* . . ." He sighed, looking right at me. "Oh, and is it *conservative*, too?" He appeared truly pained.

I pulled up my shoulders, stiffening in the chair. "Well, it would be difficult to write a memoir about becoming a Christian without mentioning Jesus," I stated matter-of-factly. "And how can it be *conservative* in the way your American tone implies? I'm Canadian, after all." I attempted a chuckle.

Grant pinned me with a look that decidedly showed he did not find anything about this conversation even remotely entertaining.

My chuckle died out and I cleared my throat.

More silence.

But I fought the temptation to fill it this time. I stayed quiet, too.

"Carolyn," he finally stated with authority, "I highly recommend that you do not write this work at all. Or if you must, that you keep it to yourself. Don't publicize it, and certainly don't include it in your progress report."

"Why not?" I had some inkling, but I wasn't prepared for the severity of his tone.

"Listen, just don't do it. Or at the very least, don't do it before you have tenure. It's just too risky, too dangerous. It would be career suicide, especially at this point in the game. It won't count toward anything, and you will have wasted your time and, worse, your reputation. Focus your energy instead on a good, solid, mainstream academic article. You've done well there; just do another one of those."

"But I don't want to . . . I can't . . ." I stammered as I tried to put the immensity of it, the urgency of it, into words.

"How about a nice little book review?" he offered frustratedly. "You'll get a half credit for that."

I just stared at him.

"Look, don't make the process so personal." Grant's admonition creaked with his chair as he leaned in even further. "Carolyn, please—do yourself, do all of us, a favor. Don't rock the boat."

I sat there not knowing how to reply, what to say.

"Dessert?" Grant attempted a lighter tone.

"No thanks." I managed a weak smile. "I've lost my appetite."

As we stood up to leave, Grant placed his hand on my arm. "Look, Carolyn," he said, more kindly this time, "I realize that much of the tenure process seems like a circus. There are certain hoops to jump through. You need to disassociate yourself from taking any of it personally and just give them what they want."

How do I not take the high-stakes assessment of a life's work—a life's passion—personally? I thought to myself as we left the table.

Then something clicked. One of those "grace insight" moments you get when the entire gestalt comes into focus, if only for a moment, but that moment illuminates a lifetime: *I can see why the evaluative world does not "get" grace*—it all came clear—*and, in turn, why grace cannot, does not, will not, conform to such human standards. You cannot "come up" for grace. You cannot qualify for it, earn it or do enough paperwork for it. No one can bestow or veto it. You can't even get it through conformity, diversity or seniority. It doesn't fit into a file, it won't tuck nicely into a page protector. It won't be laminated or promoted, bought or sold. It is a gift between God and me, and it is always here for the taking.*

Since I wasn't familiar with this campus, Grant accompanied me back to where the conference was gathering. As he left me at the door, he said over his shoulder in a lowered voice: "Nothing is worth jeopardizing everything you have worked for, all you have accumulated, all you have accomplished."

There's the beauty of it, the relentless truth of grace: even a sentence from a bureaucratic doorway can lead one through the true gate.

For, to borrow John Berger's words in reply, "sometimes to refute a single sentence it is necessary to tell a life story."[5]

When it came to faith, to say the very least, I found academia to be a conflicted place. Eventually, as I began to talk about my project, some colleagues proved openly hostile to the prospect of my writing a Christian memoir; others, however, openly cheered it on. Early in the process, I struggled: Where to begin? Was I up to the task? What if I lost everything I had worked for as a result? What if . . . what if . . . what if . . . ? Again, the old fear began to seep into the cracks. I can now see why archenemies in all the horror movies never seem to die; no matter how many times the protagonist stabs them, they somehow return. But here was the silver bullet, the stake that struck evil down so that we can get to the true heart of things: No one had warned me just how truly power-full you became when filled with the love of God. Well, I guess the prophets had. And the apostles. And my pastors. And, well, Christ himself, among us. But who *really* listens?

As I strained to hear better, I clung more fiercely to Paul's prayer for the Ephesians: "that you, being rooted and established in love, may have power, together with all the Lord's holy people, to grasp how wide and long and high and deep is the love of Christ, and to know this love that surpasses knowledge—that you may be filled to the measure of all the fullness of God" (3:17-19).

University professor Mary Poplin tells how her own newfound faith was met with skepticism, and even downright antagonism, yet she found great personal power in following God. In *Finding Calcutta*, her account of her conversion to Christianity and subsequent formative time with Mother Teresa, Poplin admits how she was not a person who cried often or easily. However, after returning to her academic work following her sabbatical ministry with Mother Teresa, she often headed to her office and burst into tears without any warning. Such uncontrollable experiences made her feel all the more vulnerable in an intellectually hostile environment.

Later, Poplin would discover Symeon, the New Theologian from the tenth century, who developed an extensive theology about tears and "believed that such tears were a gift of the Holy Spirit and that part of their purpose was to soften a hardened heart and lead a person to repentance, purification and further contemplation."[6] She realized how the Holy Spirit does some of its most poignant work through our tears. As Poplin so beautifully muses, tears are telling. The tearing tears one open to the place of no more tears. And so the telling becomes the living of the gift of the present. The Living Word becomes living the word.

I just didn't expect the cleaving to God, and the grieving for the world, to be so painful.

But then again, I also didn't see how powerful tears were—these small droplets of salted water so often mistaken for weakness.

Grieving—whether it be for people (dead or still living), places, careers, an expectation gone awry or a hope seemingly lost—all tears open the way for Christ to come more completely into our lives, and for us, in turn, to come more completely into his presence.

"Pour out your heart like water in the presence of the Lord" (Lam 2:19). Our refinement magnifies his image. As we pour out our hearts like water, so he pours out his Spirit like flame (Acts 2:1-3). Though it often surprises, the Holy Spirit brings no confusion, only clarity.

The time of recovery, emotional as well as physical, after the twins' birth led to the grieving necessary to heal. For God first has poured out himself for us: body and blood and Spirit; water and cloud and flame. The pouring remains continuous, my God who was, my God who is, my God who will be, always: "And afterward, God says, I will pour out my Spirit on all people. . . . And everyone who calls on the name of the LORD will be saved" (Joel 2:28, 32).

Our calling is to call out to him. I was beginning to see how being a member of God's family meant it was all relative. When it comes to our worries and gifts and talents and abilities, we give what we can in him, through him and to him, and God knows our hearts in the giving, and the good kind of "trying." More often than not, we are surprised—and renewed—by the depths we end up plumbing within ourselves.

"Now finish the work," Paul tells us, "so that your eager willingness to do it may be matched by your completion of it, according to your means. For if the willingness is there, the gift is acceptable according to what one has, not according to what one does not have" (2 Cor 8:11-12). I wanted to finish this work, this writing as a means of better knowing him, for me.

The Jewish critic George Steiner proposes in his book *Real Presences* that our communication is underwritten by the "assumption of God's presence."[7] But what I love about God, and am most humbled and amazed by, is his assumption of *our presence* in his communication with us: his communion with us in the dignity and delight of offering us his grace. How are we to respond to such a present but with the full presence of ourselves?

This gift of true magi, of authentic wise men, regardless of culture or age or time: this mutual communion of communication involves our presenting of our very selves in God's presence. And the gift's worth arises from the giving. As Edmund Vance Cooke put so poetically in "The Spirit of the Gift":

It is not the weight of jewel or plate,
Or the fondle of silk or fur;
'Tis the spirit in which the gift is rich,
As the gifts of the Wise Ones were,
And we are not told whose gift was gold,
Or whose was the gift of myrrh.[8]

3

Refined like Silver

Batter my heart, three-personed God; for you
As yet but knock, breathe, shine, and seek to mend;
That I may rise and stand, o'erthrow me, and bend
Your force to break, blow, burn, and make me new.

JOHN DONNE

Trauma prepares us for resurrection.

The day and the door close behind me as I walk into my house, so very different now in this winter than when I left for the hospital just last fall. Everything around me appears the same, yet everything within in me has changed as a result of this renewed calling of "Convert!"

Seattle rarely experiences many flurries at all, let alone snowfalls resulting in accumulations beyond an inch or two. Yet when a freak snowstorm hit that winter, I realized that having twins resembles waking up to just such an unexpected snowstorm. While you knew the weather report somewhat in advance, nothing can quite prepare you for the actual flurry. Add two more children under three to the mix and you pretty much have a whiteout. The blizzard becomes a sort of pathetic fallacy for your dementia of exhaustion. You can barely see straight in front of you, and the blizzard of busyness around you creates a dizzying effect.

Growing up in the Great White North, I remember hearing stories about pioneers who had to run a rope or clothesline from their house door to their barn or shed, so they could find their way in the blinding snow to tend to their animals or reach a firewood supply. In these wintry furies, the streets are a mess: traffic halts, letters sit on a mound of snow *inside* the mailbox, indoor pipes freeze. No matter what you do, the snowy onslaught keeps coming and you can't stay on top of it. Everything shuts down. Existential angst builds as you shovel and shovel without effect, much like a frostbitten Sisyphus pushing a great snowball up the hill only to have it roll back down, and over you.

How do we find our way in the chaos?

I considered hanging a clothesline from my bedroom to the nursery for those nighttime trips resulting from the demands of newborn twins.

But it was the inner, not the outer, weather that most terrified me. Being cut open literally caused the inner me to pour out. Even as Christians we can lose our way. We all lose our bearings. How to find God in the snowstorm, I found myself wondering.

Countless snowflakes whirling outside the window mirror the dizzying effect of our daily addictions to the opiate of busyness. And then there comes that pause . . . when the snow stops swirling and the wind dies down. When you open your back door, or rather, push and push on it until you can shimmy a small wedge into the dune of snow that has accumulated. And then you stand in a small triangle of space, the heat of the house on your back and the cold of the winter on your face, and you hold your breath at the settling.

Suspended.

For a moment, seeing—sensing—how white does indeed hold all colors at once.

For, if you are not still, if you do not stop and listen, you will miss the hush of newly fallen snow. The sight of it powdering the evergreens. The delicate icing of branches so that the barren trees are given life renewed and stretch their glistening arms in a nudity blown from glass.

I look at my sleeping babes with the same willing suspension of disbelief.

Part of the glory of a swirling snow, I think, is that you cannot possibly count all the snowflakes. Yet we know that each one has its own distinct pattern, a personal fingerprint. Not everything that counts can be counted, said Albert Einstein, a man who lived intimately with numbers, and science, and wonder.

Irreverence begins in not paying attention. And yet, I think, it can also stem from counting too often and too closely. The eternal cannot be insisted into a measurement. The snowstorm reminds us of this. Eventually, it pricks our want for clear sky, our ache for the star by which to mark our journey. We crave the wisdom of settled clarity, especially from within the flurry of beauty that startles and quiets.

The evening, I now noticed, settles too, as softly as the snow. The flurries have lessened in the streetlamp glow, which competes with a rising moon over the harbor empty of sailboats below. "Slowly, silently, now the moon," as Walter de la Mare writes, "Walks the night in her silver shoon; / This way, and that, she peers, and sees / Silver fruit upon silver trees."[1] I study the silvered branches of trees frozen in surprise. The usually bustling city, unprepared when it comes to snowplowing, comes to a halt. Classes get canceled and shops close. Nature, used to merely damp cold, shudders in the rarity of actual ice. Outside my window, a crystallized world sleeps. Everything is wrapped in a chrysalis, at once clear and concealed.

What is this sudden wintering? This silvering of everything to an apparent stop?

Many images of silver in Scripture become symbols of selling oneself out: Joseph's brothers selling him into slavery, or Jesus betrayed by Judas with a kiss and some coins. We give up the dearest of possessions for pocket change.

But when we ourselves become refined like silver to the glory of God, the transformation pays back what has been lost or owed. We are not yet "gold"; that awaits the restoration of all things. On this side of heaven, the closest we can become is silvered. We gain this gleam from walking with the God who walks with us, and giving him back the glory and the praise. Our silvering reflects him to a world much in need of reflection.

This first calling to follow Christ breaks us in as believers. Once we step over the line, we gain the perspective, and then we have ample opportunity to keep growing from there. And thus the beautiful gyre into the abundant life begins: to keep on converting—turning around, as the word implies, deeper and higher and greater, all through the various presents of this life.

The second calling pushes us further, challenges us more profoundly, and then rewards us far more richly than any reality we could have imagined for ourselves, on our own. The roots spread deeper, the seedling unfurls higher. And so it goes. Shoot upon shoot coming out new. The growth comes fast and furious: thick and green and lush. The result glories with sheen bright—a verdant life of the soul.

The lion's den, the crucible, the cold tomb: each offers a second calling. It may come in nudges or whispers, crises or shouts; regardless, these subsequent callings probe us both further into and out of ourselves. In each direction, they bring us closer to God. And, I have found, they make the Bible even more alive. The Word of God becomes increasingly relevant in its reverence. We know this refinement, too, to be true, for "the words of the LORD are flawless, like silver purified in a crucible, like gold refined seven times" (Ps 12:6).

Some crucibles work by heat, others by cold. Some by flame, others by water. We are compressed by too much, or we are cut loose by too little. We burn under pressure or freeze in isolation. Regardless of inner or outer weather, the effect is the same: the extremes in experiences gauge the extremes in our spiritual temperatures. Often the differences in extreme shake us out of the "in" of indifference. We are forced "out," we are forced through and beyond, we are thrust into the realm of the absolute other—from the personal and particular of self into the infinite and all of God.

Why?

Jesus does not want us to be mediocre, to be lukewarm. Indifference is literally revolting to him. "So," Jesus tells the church in Laodicea, "because you are lukewarm—neither hot nor cold—I am about to spit you out of my mouth. You say, 'I am rich; I have acquired wealth and do not need a thing.' But you do not realize that you are wretched, pitiful, poor, blind and naked. I counsel you to buy from me gold refined in the fire, so you can become rich; and white clothes to wear, so you can cover your shameful nakedness; and salve to put on your eyes, so you can see" (Rev 3:16-18). We are burned and frozen so that we may find him in our midst; but, as with Job, our true lives are never completely lost. Instead, they are burnished and restored all the more for the leaning into the gleaning, the gathering of him to us. Even in bits and pieces. Even when we're only in pursuit of a visionary gleam—a comet's tail of which we refuse to let go.

"For you, O God, tested us; you refined us like silver. . . . We went through fire and water, but you brought us to a place of abundance" (Ps 66:10-12).

I try to remember this within the snowstorm.

Kent turns on the bath for the children upstairs. Warming myself by the radiator in the foyer, I listen as the rush of water through pipes rattles the old house. Ghostly branches diamonded in snow frame the bay window.

My own spindly tree depends upon the hands of the gardener, who nurtures it and prunes it with care into a mighty oak whose branches embrace the sky. Similarly, I grow more precious in the skilled craftsmanship of the silversmith who stays with me, who turns me over and over— but never leaves me to the flames. "He will sit as a refiner and purifier of silver; he will purify the Levites and refine them like gold and silver" (Mal 3:3).

A silversmith must sit patiently and hold the metal to the fire with care. High temperatures volatize impurities in the metal and allow dross to come to the surface, so that it can be removed. But if the metal becomes too hot, the luster is destroyed. A skilled silversmith knows the purification is done when he can see his own image.[2]

Batter my heart, three-personed God; for you
As yet but knock, breathe, shine, and seek to mend;
That I may rise and stand, o'erthrow me, and bend
Your force to break, blow, burn, and make me new.

There is an art to the image making. A mirror results from glass tinged with silver.

How do we stand "new" when we are broken? When we are bent, blown, burned . . . what comes to our surface? I am moved by the praise song at church a few days later. My soul responds to the plea to God: "Break my heart for what breaks yours." I want to be made into his image, but I fear getting burned.

This birth of my twins, this crucible moment in my marriage, cracked both my husband and me open so wide and set in motion a change so radical as to reorient our entire lives. Together, our shared trauma brought to the surface other traumas, some long buried, some oh so hard to even speak—surfaced them and purged them and volatized the impurities. The process, the trusting, deepened our faith and gave us a newly won perspective, a brighter, clearer vision. Most of all, it gave us a greater conviction of the absolute restoration to come.

There are times in life, as death and near-death show us most poignantly, when you finally fully realize that you can't take anything with you. Not even a slender power bar. Not even credentials, or knowledge, or feeling. And that is when you are laid the most bare so he can do the most work. As Brennan Manning states, "It is only the reality of death that is powerful enough to quicken people out of the sluggishness of everyday life and into an active search for what life is really about."[3] We quicken in the world like babes in the womb. We move about, within and without, anxious to live, eager to be. Wired to love and be loved, within a story that has meaning beyond measure, that overflows into the infinite.

Trauma teaches you that *life is precious.* The very here and now is precious, insofar as it is melting back toward its original dignity and glory: being made in the image of God. Our hesitation to live it to the fullest in God blemishes the gift with "impurities," including, as the metaphysical poets often named it, "the sin of fear." This sin of fear prevents us from accepting grace's full payment for our refinement. When we "burn for God" we realize that life, which can otherwise seem a string of random, transient and meaningless moments, is actually *momentous* in God's eternal economy. As a result, we come to fully see that *others' lives are precious too.*

Put another way, in the hands of the faithful and exacting silversmith, we *appreciate.* We grow in value and we grow in thanks. Gratitude and worth are interlinked in worship and praise, in the purpose of our lives and the reason for our being. G. K. Chesterton declares, "I would maintain that thanks are the highest form of thought, and that gratitude is happiness doubled by wonder." In the final act of redemption, God offers his very death to help us see the Real. And in doing so, we enter a whole new life currency: a redeemed silver, electric and eternal, the aliveness of righteousness and oneness with him that is opposite of deadness in sin and isolation from him.

Disinterest must necessarily involve disintegration. It is partial and wanting, not whole and fulfilled. When we are apathetic, we are unremarkable, because we remark nothing ourselves, or worse, nothing but ourselves. But grasping the reality of Christ shocks our eyes wide open to what Manning calls "the spirituality of wonder," which "knows the world is charged with grace, that while sin and war, disease and death are terribly real, God's loving presence and power in our midst are even more real."[4]

In his retelling of the Cupid and Psyche myth, *Till We Have Faces,* C. S. Lewis offers a compassionate and challenging perspective from the point of view of a split soul. He presents us with Orual, the ugly older sister of the beautiful younger sister Psyche. In imaginatively recasting their relationship, Lewis examines how when our fragmented selves are brought back together through grace, we become capable of seeing Love for what it really is, and for how it abounds, and will overcome.

The Greek word *psyche* stood for both "soul" and "butterfly." Innate in the etymology lurks a metamorphosis from lowly creature to winged being. Lived grace leads to lives transformed. We can see the effects, but the process remains a mystery. The chrysalis through which we can only see darkly hangs from the tree on this side of paradise. To quote Lewis's Orual as she reunites with Psyche and the two sisters blend into one beautiful and everlasting being: "Joy silenced me."[5]

Lewis has Orual close her two-part narrative while dying with the following words: "I ended my first book with the words *no answer*. I know now, Lord, why you utter no answer. You are yourself the answer."[6]

We are all Psyche. We are all on this journey of the soul. We can accuse and blame and dodge and dismiss. We can even use love to ill-intentioned ends. We make golden calves of everything—careers, gifts, ministry, family members, dear ones, things that might otherwise seem noble and well intentioned—except that which we should serve first. We are not safe from ourselves. And so we are brought into the fire, where, God says, "I will refine them like silver and test them like gold. They will call on my name and I will answer them; I will say, 'They are my people,' and they will say, 'The LORD is our God'" (Zech 13:9).

To call on the Lord and to be answered.

The moon glistens far above the branches now, a silver coin tossed in a murky sky.

Broken, blown, burned and made anew, I see now how silvered silence is an answer.

4

U-Turn Friends

Christ be with me, Christ within me,
Christ behind me, Christ before me,
Christ beside me, Christ to win me,
Christ to comfort and restore me,
Christ beneath me, Christ above me,
Christ in quiet, Christ in danger,
Christ in hearts of all that love me,
Christ in mouth of friend and stranger.

<small>PRAYER OF ST. PATRICK</small>

A year later, after I successfully received tenure and completed my remaining teaching requirements, we arrived in Santa Barbara for my sabbatical. The boys were toddling and talking now, running in two different directions at once. I would be using the relative seclusion here to finally complete the writing of my conversion story. I prepared to settle into my usual self-sufficiency, but again, the Lord had other plans for me.

"What a friend we have in Jesus!"

Sitting there in a new church, the congregation sang alive the long-enduring hymn, written by Joseph Scriven in 1855. In music, the words soared above me, beautiful and genuine. But it wasn't always that way. Before I was a Christian, the line had stung. *How can we have a friend we cannot even see?* I used to think. *I mean, come on, who swallows this stuff?* It seemed the ether that swirly-eyed hippies were made of, something that someone at a commune might say trying to convince you that the end of the world was coming so we all better give each other a hug. Or worse, what a placard-waving zealot might sing out to an innocent bystander who just lost the love of his life, trying to convince him that the world is just and right and good anyway.

It bugged me.

Even later, as a believer, the line when extracted and tossed about as cliché still owned the power to make me wince. It seemed so, well, happy-clappy, feel-goodie, canned-cheesy, sing-songs-around-the-campfire. Ugh.

Trite or truth?

I soon began to see, however, that the question applied to me. And the answer lay within being friends in Jesus.

During that first year in Santa Barbara, many of these manifestations of his love for me through others in him came in the form of a headache.

Yes, a headache.

A migraine, to be exact.

Shortly after we arrived in Santa Barbara, and for the first time in my life, I experienced a migraine. At first, I had no idea what was happening. Kent had just left on a twenty-four-hour trip back to Seattle to manage outgoing and incoming tenants at our home on the first of the month. The holiday timing stunk; it was actually New Year's Eve Day. I hadn't been feeling well when I drove him to the airport, but shrugged it off, blaming a bug or perhaps something I ate—nothing that getting an early night once the kids were down and perhaps taking an aspirin or two wouldn't fix.

A few hours later I found myself back at home, heaving my guts out in the bathroom with the kids clinging helplessly to my legs. My head spun like a carousel of evil steeds on speed, and I couldn't open my eyes to the light. It felt like someone had swung an ax through the left side of my brain. It was growing increasingly difficult to form words or make controlled movements. Was this a stroke? Had I unwittingly ingested some sort of poison? I had never experienced anything like it.

My heart swung in terror. This was my worst nightmare come true in real time: being left alone with my children, helpless, with something terrible happening to me, leaving me unable to take care of them. I feared collapsing, being blacked out for days, my little ones running around, unsupervised, uncared for, and somehow finding their way out of the house . . .

Actually, when I look back at it now, an unleashing of my children poses much more of a risk to others than to themselves. But hey, I was still a nervous young mom, after all.

Besides, I didn't know a single neighbor. Because of the holiday, virtually nothing was open. There was not even a medical hotline to call. I could hear party revelers starting to make their way down to the beach as the sun fell lower in the sky. People laughed and drank in their yards all around us; in one of the most beautiful beach towns in the world, I existed in a crowd but had never felt so alone. Having been here only a short time, we didn't belong to a community yet and had only just begun attending church on the recommendation of a good friend back in Seattle.

A single local contact lurked in my cell phone: the church's youth director, a friendly young woman with piercing blue eyes and a head full of dancing curls. I gut-liked her right away. But could I really call such a new acquaintance out of the blue, with such a random request for help? What would she think? Could I really trust her with my children? My mind raced, well, more like limped, through the blinding pain. Blinking in the excruciatingly sunlit living room, I herded the children like miscreant alley cats onto the couch and managed to turn on a cartoon.

Then I vomited some more, which always, for a moment at least, has a clarifying effect.

Okay, I said to myself. *You have no other options here. Friendless relocated beggars can't be high safety choosers.* In blinding pain, I clicked down my phone's contacts to the youth director's name. Forever seared now in a memory of gratitude, every time I even think of her name, it appears within that cell phone glow: *Lisa.*

I heard the numbers dial. One ring. What if she doesn't pick up? Two rings. What if she's a crazy person? Three rings. Or worse—what if I she thinks I'm a crazy person and doesn't call back? Fourth ring . . .

"Hello?" a voice brightly asked.

My heart sang at the sound of such sweetness.

"Hi, um, Lisa?"

"Yes."

"This is Carolyn . . ." I stopped, retched into the kitchen sink, then tried to speak again: "Uh . . ."

"Are you okay?" Lisa suddenly sounded concerned.

I swallowed back the next wave in attempt of a feeble reply: "That's actually why I'm calling . . ."

"Oh my goodness, what is it? How can I help?" I could feel her kindness wash in like a current through the telephone connection.

In a few stunted sentences, punctuated by retches, I tried to explain my situation in a pain-garbled daze.

Lisa spoke reassuringly, with a compassionate and calm air. "Hold on, Carolyn. I'll be right there."

INSERT ANGELS SINGING HERE.

I gripped the counter to steady myself, partly from the pain, but partly from being carried over and out of myself by the soaring music of such deep and unexpected kindness.

I'll be right there.

And indeed, she is *right there.* Before the call, the minutes seemed to stretch into hours as I stood alone and afraid in my tiny kitchen, anxious children swarming my knees. But it seems that as soon as I set down the phone, there is a knock at the door. Lisa sweeps in, takes one look at me, gasps and then catches herself, turns on her heels and starts packing the kids into the car. Sensing my sensitive older daughter's apprehension, Lisa speaks in an upbeat yet authoritative tone to the kids: "All right, everyone. We are going to take a fun ride to the hospital. Mommy needs a little help, and we are going to make sure she gets there safely."

"But I don't want to go the hospital," Victoria whines. "I want to watch the end of *The Little Mermaid.*"

The boys, still struggling for vocabulary, sip their apple juice in a unified stance, refusing to budge from the couch. *Who is this person?* Their little faces look at me quizzically.

I manage to mumble a few words of agreement, encouraging them toward the car. I then tumble into the front passenger's seat.

Lisa puts a bowl in my lap and a towel at my feet. She buckles the children in and drives us to the hospital, which requires getting on the freeway (I wouldn't even know how to get there yet in this strange town). She reaches over to pat my hand reassuringly whenever she is not on her cell phone.

For on her cell phone she gets, and wow, what a force! It is like riding with Jesus on an iPhone. She throws in a church music CD for the kids, blasts the air conditioner for me, then begins with precision to demon dial (if you'll pardon the expression here) several numbers with ease, one after the other. In a few moments, she has lined up someone to meet me at the hospital and check me in while she tends the kids in the car, someone else to drive me home when I check out, someone to drop by and pray with me, someone to help her with the kids tomorrow, as she explains she will plan to stay the night.

Who are all these people? I wonder to myself. "Wait," I try to get out, "*stay the night?*" But the words are lost in the echo of the bowl on my lap. From what I piece together, they are folks in the church, believing friends of hers, youth group kids she serves. Each one is willing to jump at a moment's notice to help. To help a *stranger*. To help a *vomiting stranger*. To help a *vomiting stranger with three very small and maniacal children.*

In awe, I peer out over my bowl at her profile. It is like overhearing a series of conversations across the CB: trucks all in communication with each other on the highway of life. Truck drivers for Christ, all plugged into the other type of CB, the Christian Brotherhood station, giving hitchhikers a lift, filling each other's tanks, stopping to fix the broken-down and flat-tired.

Imagine the relief of having the woman from Proverbs 31 at the wheel! Calm and cool and collected, Lisa gathers sources from afar. I notice her strong arms. Good for making U-turns with.

Which we actually do, a few times, on the way to the hospital, given some of the obstacles that pop up on our way. With the exacting speed of a racecar driver, Lisa weaves us through California traffic on the freeway toward the hospital exit.

When we screech into the ER parking lot, a severe-looking security guard approaches us, telling us that we cannot park there. We are not blocking any route. Lisa explains our situation quickly.

"Sorry, ma'am," the officer interrupts, leaning into the driver's window menacingly, "it's standard procedure. You cannot park here." He directs her to park several blocks down, in a building.

Lisa, who looks like a woman from a Botticelli painting, all soft tresses spilling about her shoulders, turns in her seat completely toward him and states with a menace matching his, "Oh yes, we can, sir. This woman is ill, and I have a car full of kids in here! Your standards stink and procedures will have to wait."

I emphasize her point by puking into my bowl. The children begin wailing. Once in a while—not often, mind you—but once in a great while, their timing is impeccable that way.

He backs away from the window, drop-jawed.

"Watch the kids while I get her admitted!" she calls out to him as she smacks the gear into park.

"Yes, ma'am," he says respectfully as he opens her door, and then comes around to get mine.

A few other cars begin to pull in; I realize they are her contacts just starting to arrive. Lisa calls over a friend to watch the kids and move the car to a better location until she can join them shortly. She introduces me to this friend, then tucks a blanket around me and helps me into the wheelchair the security guard offers. A good thing, too, as my shakes have become so bad that I cannot feel my extremities.

By the time I am wheeled in, the pain is beyond excruciating; I now own a whole new level of compassion for those who suffer from migraines.

"What about my kids—" I begin to ask, but a nurse hushes me to take my blood pressure.

"It's all under control." Lisa smiles at me over her shoulder as she turns to head back to the car. "Don't you worry, just concentrate on getting well. Now that you are in good hands, I'll get the kids all settled in safely with one of my absolute best friends here and I'll be back in a jiffy."

All I can do is look at her with puppy-eyed gratitude as the swinging doors close between us, and between me and my kids in the hands of this stranger. To whom I am a stranger, too—I realize. Except that we have Christ in common. Though she would have done the same for me if I hadn't been a believer. The onus in loving one another, I begin to see, falls on the one most capable at that moment in Christ. And as Scripture teaches us, being the only one present in Christ automatically qualifies you for the most responsibility.

Testing these waters of fellowship, I am beginning to learn, oh me of little faith, that when you indeed have a friend in Jesus, there are no strangers.

After the painkiller surges into my veins, I begin to drift . . .

The nurse leans in and takes my pulse again. "Oh honey," she croons kindly in my ear, "your heart rate betrays exhaustion." She leans in even closer. I notice she smells like the interior of the shops I used to enter when we lived near Haight-Ashbury in the hippie district of San Francisco: all incense swirled with passive rebellion. "I have studied Eastern medicine, too," she whispers close to my ear.

"Your energy, your *chi*, is normally very vital, I can tell, but right now it's out of whack."

"Oh," is all I can muster in response.

"You poor thing," she says gently. "Have you tried yoga? Burning some sage in your home? How about regular massage?"

I know she means well, and these things certainly sound lovely, I have to admit. So did the recommendations from the doctor who just prescribed my medication: "Get some extra help with the kids, the house, the meals. Get your groceries delivered, a personal assistant. Get to the spa!" But who with small children has the time? Who on leave from their job, and without any even remotely normal income, has the money?

But then I remind myself that this *is* Santa Barbara.

I drift again breathing in the nurse's potpourri. Slowly I surface—when? I do not know how much time has elapsed. I feel anchored to the cot by my heavy limbs. But I find the relentless nausea has lessened, the electrocution of my cerebral sockets is now dulled to a receding pounding. Someone is sitting in my peripheral, still slightly blurry vision. I turn my head. Bright blue eyes pierce the dim room. The outline of bouncy curls shadows on the wall. A warm smile spreads on this newly dear face, as a reassuring touch reaches out for my arm.

I remember Lisa. Term of endearment for Elizabeth. Cousin of Mary and mother of John the Baptist. Now I understood why Mary would travel such a distance, though pregnant, to see such a person. Probably precisely *because* she was pregnant. And probably feeling a touch alone, if not at least worn out, too. Urged on a pilgrimage ending in the embrace of Elizabeth.

"Your kids are fine." Lisa smiles at me before I even have the chance to speak. I settle back on my pillow, relieved. "Just rest," she says softly as she rubs my arm.

It's still difficult to form words, but now because of fatigue more than pain. I am weary. *Maybe I should consider burning some sage, or breathing in eucalyptus?* I wonder vaguely. *Anything's worth a shot.*

"Our pastor will be here shortly to take you home," Lisa explains. "I'm going to go ahead and get back to your kids. Jenn, whom you met, is with them. She's wonderful. I'm going to spend the night with them, and with you."

"Oh, I'll be okay . . . just get me home . . ." I struggle to sit up again.

"No way," she interrupts. "You are far too weak. You need to sleep off the medication and take some time to recover. It's a non-negotiable. I will stay the night and watch the kids through tomorrow. I have to shift around a few commitments, but I have a couple of friends who can cover for me tomorrow afternoon. You need some good, solid recovery time."

Inside, I almost sob at the phrase.

"But you aren't prepared . . ." I stammer.

"Oh yes I am!" Lisa chirps, pulling a feminine pair of panties from her purse with a flourish. "I threw in an extra pair of underwear!" Her laughter fills the room, its wake rocking me into sleep unafraid.

When I next wake, a fuzzy face nearby comes into view. A few blinks reveal that it belongs to the senior pastor of our new church. We have met him only a handful of times. He immediately gets up and comes to my side when he sees me try to rise. He holds my arm to help me brace myself. I look up at his kind face and am amazed that he is here. He gives me a kindhearted smile.

Then I bend over and throw up right beside his feet.

In horror, I squint, trying to see whether it splattered his shoes. He's dressed very nicely, I notice to my even greater mortification. I remember with a pang that it's New Year's Eve. I learn later that it was also the rehearsal dinner night for his son's wedding, which was the next day. Hesitantly, I look up into his face again.

To my further amazement, his smile remains. And not even in a forced way. In fact, it only broadens—genuinely.

The hippie nurse rushes over, muttering, "Honey, oh honey, you shouldn't have raised your head so quickly. You might be starting to feel better, but you've got to take it slowly." Like a small child, I allow her to nestle me back on the pillows and tuck the sheet around me. I notice she wears a small gold pendant around her neck that reads "Goddess." An apt epithet for nurses, I have to admit.

She passes my pastor a towel.

"Oh, I'm fine," he declines. "I'm used to not getting directly hit on by women." He grins with boyish charm.

The nurse laughs. "And how do you know our patient?" she asks as she brings me a bedpan.

"He's my pastor," I interject.

"Your pastor?" She looks at me wide eyed, then at him. "Wow—your pastor came? And you are not even *dying*?"

I nod yes, not willing to open my mouth any more than necessary at this point, lest more than words pour out.

"That is so cool," she drawls, in genuine admiration.

"Well, thanks," my pastor replies humbly. To me, he resembles a coin: flip it, and you see the dignified imprint of a Roman citizen on one side; flip it again, and you catch a glimpse of an impish youth with a quick smile. Pastor Don embodies that rare combination of super-smart intellect and an endearing, almost boyish energy. I have noticed that he delivers his sermons with astute exegetical acumen but hops up and down away from the pulpit when he is making a particularly passionate point. Married to a classy artist of French de-

scent, himself a savvy transplant from Minnesota, he reads vora-
ciously in a beautiful study but also swims almost daily in ice-cold
surf, unafraid of sharks. That about sums it up.

"Lisa, who was here earlier, and I," he adds, "well, we've gotten to
know Carolyn and her family through our church."

"Double wow," the nurse says with admiration. "Almost makes me
want to go to church!"

"You should give it a shot," Pastor Don winks. Then he pulls up a
chair and sits down next to me.

The doctor stops by to prescribe more fluids for my dehydration.
He looks over at my pastor, and after they nod a mutual hello, the
doctor says, "Okay, you can help your wife get undressed now."

Pastor Don goes red as the nurse explains, "He's her pastor." The
doctor raises one brow.

"My husband's out of town, and I don't know anyone else here at
all yet, really," I mumble into the metallic ricochet of the bedpan.
The effect is to increase the tinny ring of my interjected self-pity.

The doctor apologizes as he passes me a gown. Then he ducks out.

"Well, don't you have the support network!" The nurse pats my
cheek. "That is really something, especially in this day and age. Fantastic energy in here! Just love it!" She bustles out with the dirty
linens in hand. At the doorway she stops and throws my pastor a
meaningful glance: "Good karma, too!"

My pastor simply looks back at me, his eyes alight with compassion
and concern. "Whenever you are ready, I'm here to take you home."

Like the lyrics to a Beatles' song, I get by with a little help from
my friend(s) in Jesus. Is this a line that has become equally cliché?
Or did the Beatles owe more to Jesus than even John Lennon would
have cared to admit?

Karma throws everything back in your face (or nearly ruins your shoes), I thought. *No, it's grace.* It's grace that smiles even when things are lower than low. Even when another regurgitates bitterness all around you, grace smiles *broader.*

I awoke the next morning in my own bed to the sound of Lisa's sweet singing in the kitchen as she tended to my children's needs. I can still hear the children's laughter in response to her contagious joy.

And I realize, now, too, that it is grace that takes you home.

Such a fine line exists between *friend* and *fiend.* The slightest difference between *friend* and *fiend* lies in where you *r* at. Lucifer slipped from one to the other with the loss of his "are." He wanted to be God, he desired to go against what was good, overthrow what was right. And so in rejecting the all that is the "are" of heaven for the lack of hell, he lost the rank of closest friend for the title of most hurled-away fiend. Of this transition, in his timeless seventeenth-century epic *Paradise Lost,* John Milton has the fallen archangel tellingly announce: "Better to reign in Hell than serve in Heaven."[1]

The longer and more earnestly we cultivate our relationship with Jesus, the deeper and more truth-reflecting that friendship becomes. Friendships in his fellowship further reflect this communion. "The best mirror is an old friend," wisely claimed the metaphysical poet George Herbert.

So even though when we first arrived in Santa Barbara we didn't personally know a soul, the Lord brought what proved to be several what I like to call "U-turn friends" such as Lisa and other church members into my life to deepen my relationship with him. Such friends remind us of the body of Christ. They draw us into God's presence. For in making a U-turn, so to speak, out of the daily hustle and bustle of things to be exactly what we need at exactly the right time, such folks recall our Lord's life, death and resurrection for us.

A "U-turn" friend is someone who will stop whatever he is doing at the moment and immediately change direction to come and help a friend in need. Such friends turn from the demands of "me" to the service of "you." Of course, there are generous folks who will do this for a complete stranger as well. Regardless, a U-turn friend comes to your aid, especially during a storm, in the dark or times of "attack"— when we are most vulnerable. Everyone should have at least one U-turn friend. And, in turn, we should each try to be one to others. As the proverb goes, "When friends ask, there is no tomorrow." Living out the great commandment to love another as we have been loved is yet another gift of the present, and proof to others of God moving among us (Jn 13:34-35).

"Greater love has no one than this: to lay down one's life for one's friends" (Jn 15:13). Jesus epitomizes the U-turn friend. He turned his entire Godhead on its head to save our sorry behinds. And when we accept him as Lord over our lives, indeed we each have at least one U-turn friend, and the one that most matters and encompasses all others.

But the neat thing about loving Christ first, and then loving others from that first love, is how U-turn friends create U-turn friends: this is how the cycle goes. It becomes a spinning circle of grace that turns us back, ultimately, to God, as we see again later in the story of Peter. In response to Jesus' reinstating him, Peter gives his own life. Peter even turns his own death around to honor Jesus, when, after a life of ministry in his name, he insists on being crucified upside down. Thus everywhere *you* turn, Christ surrounds you through his people.

Peter was one of the first to follow Jesus, leaving his boat—his livelihood and identity—and going with the others called by Jesus' urging to follow him and "fish for people." Then later these same men would bond in a boat during a storm as Jesus himself sought rest surrounded by these handpicked friends, friends who had turned on a dime to follow him. Such friends as modeled in these first disciples echo in their human frailty the perfect friendship Jesus offers us in turning everything over to us, in giving over his life.

Similarly, the parable of the good Samaritan from Luke 10:25-37 has become a cultural cliché of sorts. But when we realize that it appears in the most serious of contexts—that is, how do we acquire eternal life?—we begin to see that the illustration Jesus gives stretches far and wide in meaning. Mercy becomes the defining factor in what qualifies someone as a "neighbor." In the ultimate judgment, "the King will reply, 'Truly I tell you, whatever you did for one of the least of these brothers and sisters of mine, you did for me'" (Mt 25:40).

Mother Teresa recognized the truthness, not triteness, in such parables when she claimed, "I believe in person to person. Every person is Christ for me, and since there is only one Jesus, that person is the one person in the world at that moment."[2] C. S. Lewis similarly discerns this holy magic of God's presence secreted within community: "Next to the Blessed Sacrament itself, your neighbor is the holiest object presented to your senses. If he is your Christian neighbor he is holy in almost the same way, for in him also Christ *vere latitat*—the glorifier and the glorified, Glory Himself, is truly hidden."[3]

How better to notice God in our lives than through his "remarkable" people?

What a friend we have in Jesus . . . what friends we have in Jesus—the tune sings differently to me now. For this is what I have learned: U-turn friends love us into undeserving understanding.

Praise him.

5

Even Jesus Went
Out in a Boat

The selfsame moment I could pray;
And from my neck so free
The Albatross fell off, and sank
Like lead into the sea.

SAMUEL TAYLOR COLERIDGE

A stormy winter season ensued. Palm leaves littered the streets from the high winds, and boats pitched and got grounded regularly on the Santa Barbara shore. In the midst of such bitter weather, the post brought news of my professional review from the university committee. My teaching and service categories, and even prior publications, had all received top ratings. But when it came to my most recent publication intersecting my faith with my profession, concerns had been raised over the "troubling direction" of my scholarship.

Troubled myself, I send a harried note to an esteemed woman in our church whom my spiritual gut told me I could trust. Diana immediately puts me in her busy schedule, a gracious "meet and treat." She meets me at a local café and treats me to a Winter Dream tea latte. To a Canadian the name of the tea offers a bit of ironic marketing in Santa Barbara, where Advent remains a consistent balmy 60 degrees. But I blissfully sip the spicy sweet anyway, breathing in the cardamom and feeling, indeed, very wintry dreamy. The effect is never quite the same after Christmas, but the taste lingers precious, perhaps because soon it will not be available at all.

Diana asks me how I am, and the landslide is launched. I show her the letters, speak of the concerns raised against me by a range of colleagues from various institutions and connections over publishing on my Christian faith. Even though I am tenured now, the blows come in relation to the politics of further promotion. I bring to the table my accumulated exhaustion from not having had an uninterrupted night of sleep in years, nor any time alone, ever, with my husband . . . I lament my helplessness at my parents' aging and ailing when I am at such a distance, I bemoan the fact that our house in which we sank all our hard work and savings won't sell in this recession . . . I complain that I cannot possibly write all those recommendation letters for decades of former students, accruing even during sabbatical, with editing deadlines looming and children who get sick in rotation . . . I sorrow over the fact that my father will most likely die soon and there is no reconciliation there . . . I keep suffering from migraines. I am weary of worrying, and trying to make it all "work." I am ashamed to admit it, but I am weary of—life.

Lava or snow? Avalanche or flood? I am heated to the boiling point, but frozen, oh so cold, somewhere deep inside. And I wonder, how does *she* do it all—this woman of faith, family and humble authority?

We sit, two heads nearly touching, at a two-seater back table drenched in sunlight while celebrities surreally waltz in and out with their lattes. I finally take a breath, if only to refuel. To my surprise, more pours out. I admit to her I have recurring dreams of sleeping— just sleeping—in a bed with high-thread-count percale sheets in a luxury hotel without my husband, without anyone, just me and a bed and oh! so glorious room service! And when I add (guiltily) that I wake up almost weeping at the dissolution of the dream, she just smiles gently at me. Then she says, "You know it's bad when you dream about sleeping."

I nod, then take another breath and tell her how when I drive the vertigo back roads ribboning mountainside along ocean (at those rare times when I'm actually alone in the car), I sometimes contemplate how the smallest jerk in the wheel would plunge me so serenely into never-ending blue . . .

And then I could sleep. *Just sleep.*

We sit there together, in silence.

Her smile fades and she gives me an intense look.

"A sort of Thelma and Louise. But just Thelma. Or Louise." I try a pathetic joke. I am half joking.

She doesn't laugh, but she doesn't admonish either. Instead, she just leans in closer (a tendency I've come to admire in those of deep faith who interact with others who need to tap into that reservoir). She takes my hands in her beautiful older ones and says my name softly, "Oh Caro," like a prayer. I feel the pressure of her wedding band against mine. Then she speaks seven words that have stayed with me ever since:

"Even Jesus went out in a boat."

I blink at her. Then I pull out my hands and slug back more caffeine. Yes. Our Lord gets away from the crowds, the demands. He goes out with his close circle of friends and, well, sleeps. Though his sleep tends to get interrupted, too.

Okay, I nod slowly at this dear lady before me. But then I snap into the defense.

"Are you suggesting—? But I can't take a trip. I can't go away!" The panic rises with my voice. "Certainly not alone. The house would fall apart. Kent would feed the kids nachos for dinner every night. I'd be a horrible mother. What about that stack of reference letters for all those graduating students? I'll ruin their lives if I don't get them mailed in time—and then there are those deadlines for my editor... And what about the social commitments, the appointments, ugh, the housework..."

But what I really wanted to say was *Who will do everything if I don't?*

As though reading my mind, Diana responds. "You don't have to do it all, and you certainly don't have to do it all on your own. Besides," she gives a chuckle, "it doesn't have to be forty days, you know. It might only be forty minutes, say, or as long as it takes a storm to pass. Time to be alone with God. Even just a few committed moments create a discipline of presence. Inner retreat, regardless of outer circumstances, is a gift worth pursuing."

I throw her a wary look. She matches it with a knowing one. This dear, older, wiser lady who has raised children, and buried one by marriage; who has loved her family and her ministry—and most of all, her God—hard. Even when she wasn't in the mood (another trait of deep Christians I've come to admire greatly).

I try breathing her in with the cardamom. I think of frankincense and myrrh: the fragrances I imagine spiritual gold must emanate.

"It's okay to retreat, Caro," she says as takes my hands again. "God still knows where to find us."

—— ❁ ——

Outside my little kitchen, the palm trees bend almost all the way over like lithe acrobats tossed by the winter winds. Rain pelts the window as I refill the kettle and set it back on the burner, clicking the gas starter until it lights. While the Californian winter by no means approaches the arctic effect of my northern origins, the weather still grows chill and damp, often even stormy for weeks on end, and it can get quite cold along the Santa Barbara shoreline, especially inside the older beach houses with their paltry heating.

The children have grown restless from days trapped in the small, chilly house. There exist relatively few indoor options here, given the otherwise pretty much perfect weather. For now at least, they busy themselves making tents out of blankets and pillows in the front room. I grab the rare opportunity to make a second cup of tea. I pull up a chair at the kitchen table, blow the postpartum dust off my Bible and open it to the story of when Jesus calms the storm, so appropriate to return to given Diana's recent words and the wind's furious rant rattling our side door.

The outer weather reminds me of the inner. When it comes to resonating with our soulscapes, there is none other like the Bible. Looking at the passage before me now, I see just how fitting it is that when Jesus goes out in a boat, alone with his disciples, no fair-weather trip takes place. A storm wells up, and not just any storm but a sudden and mighty one: the ultimate terror to fishermen at sea.

Both Matthew and Mark include this story in their Gospels. Each of them emphasizes how Jesus left behind the pressing crowds to cross the lake, to be alone with just his small circle of disciples. This boat ride is clearly a retreat for him, after an intense period of teaching and healing thronged by crowds. In Mark's version (4:35-

41), the story is preceded by the parable of the mustard seed, in which the smallest grain of faith can produce the largest of all trees. Matthew emphasizes even more heavily the many miracles Jesus performs before his boat trip. We are reminded of the exhaustion even our Lord must have felt when, just before crossing the lake, he replies to one eager to follow him: "Foxes have dens and birds have nests, but the Son of Man has no place to lay his head" (Mt 8:20). Where is God himself to rest?

The story of Jesus' calming the storm is the only time in the Gospels I am aware of when we see Jesus sleep. Obviously, the pace of his ministry takes a toll on his humanity. After expending such energy and ministering such care, he quite simply needs to rest. But the story also illustrates Jesus' dependence on and submission to the heavenly Father in another way. We are at our most vulnerable in our sleep. By falling asleep peacefully in the boat as the storm rages all around, Jesus shows ultimate and complete trust in his Father, and thus enjoys inner rest and rejuvenation regardless of outer circumstance.

But cradled in the boat rocked on restless waves, he also rests among his U-turn friends.

In her discussion of Rembrandt's painting of this scene, *Christ in the Storm on the Lake of Galilee*, Juliet Benner unpacks further the repercussions of Jesus' response to his disciples:

> His question to them about their lack of faith is an invitation to them to abandon control, to trust him completely and not be afraid. His question to them is also a question to us in whatever distress we might be experiencing. "Why do you fear? Why do you have no faith? How long will you wait before turning to me for help?" Far from being uncaring or aloof, Jesus is actually in the boat with his disciples. He is in our boat too.[1]

Even God as man needed time away from the crowds; even Jesus required rest. But it was his faith that rocked him to sleep, heedless of the storm that rocked his disciples' confidence. I needed to remember that Jesus was in my boat, and that it was okay to retreat to regain my rest in that knowledge, before I landed on the other bank.

I think of my fellow believers, those here teaching me so much about being able to rest in friendship and retreat. When we give to God, he replenishes us in return. And the grace of it all is that he often does so even when we haven't given, or haven't given all that much. I'm living proof. He fills our jars, bowls, wells. Any sacrifice, if we can deem it such, that we make to him is rendered a thousandfold in return. Hands reach out to help us walk on the waves; we do not rock in the boat alone.

The story of the woman and the jars of oil from 1 Kings demonstrates just this replenishing in God, via his faithful servants—in this case, the prophet Elijah. God sends Elijah to Zarephath, instructing him to stay and eat with a widow there. However, when Elijah arrives, he finds the widow desperate. When he asks her for a little water and bread, she replies: "As surely as the LORD your God lives, I don't have any bread—only a handful of flour in a jar and a little olive oil in a jug. I am gathering a few sticks to take home and make a meal for myself and my son, that we may eat it—and die" (17:12).

I get the sense that this lady may have had moments of wanting to drive off a cliff, too. Elijah tells her to make a small cake of bread for him, and then something for her and her son. He assures her that the jar of flour and the jug of oil will not run out. The widow obeys, and the Lord provides them with enough food every day; "the jar of flour was not used up and the jug of oil did not run dry" (1 Kings 17:16).

The kettle whistles angrily and I get up to make more tea. The winds have quieted and so have the children, who rest now too, albeit from their hyperplay, wrapped in the debris of their collapsed tents, flipping through picture books. I watch the storm wane as I hold my cup and blow ripples across the steaming liquid. Soon the reprieve will come, and I will go for a walk outside with once coiled-up children now unsprung. Together we will pick up large palm branches that have fallen, littering the damp ground like massive quills. Then we will return home, waving them triumphantly. A small parade of *hosanna*: a calling for help and of praise.

6

Carpe Deum

He who bends to himself a joy
Doth the winged life destroy,
But he who kisses the joy as it flies
Lives in Eternity's sunrise.

WILLIAM BLAKE

There are some vistas so perfect that they almost hurt the soul with their glory.

The view this day was one of those: the kind that pierces us with longing for our eternal home.

But for now, it was hard to imagine we would soon be returning to our earthly home in Seattle. I stood on the beach in Santa Barbara, California, just down the curve in the road from our little rental house on the mesa. It was an unusually warm day for spring, even in the more temperate parts of California. Shielding my eyes from the sun's brilliance with my hand over my brow, I gazed out at the expanse of deep blue sea swelling against a flawless pale blue sky. The water ebbed and flowed toward my toes, buried in cornstarch-soft sand. Gulls gently kited in the lilting wind.

Laughter surrounds me as my children chase each other, digging in the sand and playing in the surf.

I fanned out my beach blanket and pinned down each corner with a rock. Kicking off my flip-flops, I sat down squarely in the middle of the flower print and propped my beach bag behind the small of my back for support. Sighing, I settled in for a desperately needed moment of restoration.

When I woke up this morning, as on so many—too many— mornings, to-dos and tasks were on my mind. Endless pages of paperwork balanced in cockeyed heaps on my desk. My laundry pile had grown so high that the children were playing hide-and-seek in it. The fridge yawned bare when I opened it to retrieve milk for my coffee. So many things called for my attention that when my children's voices also rose in plaintive tones of beckoning, an entire sea of demands swirled around me, threatening to swallow me whole.

"Mommy, please oh please, let's go to the beach today!" my daughter chirped over her cereal.

I hesitated, noticing that the laundry pile had grown tentacles that were now reaching out into the hall.

"*Please, Mom, please!*" all three children cried in unison, clanging breakfast spoons in demand.

"Quiet down!" I yelled, in one of those usual parental oxymorons. Like when I told my three-year-old to stop acting like a three-year-old, or when I shouted at them in the car to stop shouting. I needed another cup of coffee before I could make any kind of decision, let alone one that put off being responsible. I needed a self-help group for caffeine addiction. Badly.

The children stilled, waiting with large, round liquid eyes— spaniel eyes—pinned on me.

I avoided the canine-sympathy stare and peeked through the window behind them. It had been dreary these last few weeks. I was sure that the weather would support the necessity of completing, or at least pecking at, the greatest of all existentialist documents: a mother's to-do list. But as luck would have it for the kids, the pathetic fallacy of my window view supported their claim on the day over mine, I had to admit.

The sky stunned blue, without a trace of cloud. Slender palm trees swayed in the softest of breezes. I recalled our old Seattle stomping grounds at this time of year: gray and damp swirled with mushy dark. Much as I imagined a giant's bowl of gruel in a fairytale. Locals joked that the sun didn't show up until the July Fourth weekend. Certainly in May, the opening of boating season held no guarantee of a pleasant forecast. In fact, for the eight years we had lived there, each Boat Day had been plagued by inclement weather. Umbrellas dotted the shore as boaters set doggedly forth beneath foggy, drizzling clouds. Eeyore weather, I inwardly called it. But as I looked out from our little beachside house on this California mesa, today's forecast was definitely all Tigger. My heart leaped with it.

Three faces hung in suspended anticipation of my answer. You could have heard a Cheerio drop.

From the silence, a favorite poem of my mom's emerged. She used to recite it to us often by heart. Essentially raising us on her own, my mom still found the time to pack the car for the beach and take us as often as her work schedule and the weather allowed. With her meager means, we still somehow stopped for double-decker ice-cream cones, chins dripping with not one but two—*two*—flavors of our choice from the old-fashioned Ice Cream Shoppe on the way.

No, on a beautiful warm day when she didn't have to go to work, shopping for diapers or folding laundry never trumped my mom's heart-filled pilgrimage to the beach.

Later, when I studied Latin, I already recognized the phrase as the title to this poem:

It's too much trouble to go to the beach.
We'll wait for another day,
When the floors are scrubbed
And the clothes are washed
And everything's put away.
And then one day my work was done—
"Let's go to the beach," I said.
And I looked outside, the wind was cold
And summer's leaves were red.
And I looked around for those golden heads
But the children, too, had flown.
And I know that now if I go at all
I'll go to the beach alone . . .[1]

Carpe diem—or "seize the day!"—as the old saying goes, usually attributed to Horace. In some respects, the phrase has morphed into cultural cliché, or sadly, even an excuse to justify any type of irresponsible behavior or whim. Robert Herrick's seventeenth-century poem endures today as well, the first stanza in particular offering an often-quoted image of plucking all we can from the moment:

Gather ye rosebuds while ye may,
Old time is still a-flying;
And this same flower that smiles to-day,
Tomorrow will be dying.[2]

Live in the moment! Glorify youth! Act whenever you can, without care or investment. The phrase bears a good reminder of our mortality, and thus the call to enjoy things the first (and often only) time around. But it can teeter into hedonism. Should this fleeting life be about doing what we please? Does our mortality justify anything done in the moment to serve this pleasure principle? In the popular movie *Dead Poets Society*, the passionate literature teacher John Keating (whose name obviously evokes the Romantic poet who died at a young age, John Keats), played by Robin Williams, delivers what has become one of the most famous set of lines in American film history: "*Carpe diem*. Seize the day, boys. Make your lives extraordinary!" Jumping up on the desk and shouting with intent gives off a certain contagious spark. But sparks grow into infernos, and so how do we best tend the flames?

Perhaps the answer lies in when *carpe diem* evokes worship, when it is a form of honoring the God who is honoring us with his presence. Put another way, when *carpe diem* becomes *carpe Deum*, or, translated loosely for our purposes here, "seize God!" Scripture constantly reminds us to seize God. We see this in the story of Martha and Mary (Lk 10:38-42). Or when Jesus defends Mary to his disciples when she pours expensive oil on his feet, declaring: "You will always have the poor among you, but you will not always have me" (Jn 12:2-8). Or when Jesus challenges customs about the Sabbath, introducing a new way of understanding the holy in the present: his disciples eat the grain from the field as they pass, Jesus heals the sick, and he reminds the Pharisees of how David even helped himself to the consecrated bread in the temple, literally the "bread of the presence" (Mt 12:1-13). Why? "For the Son of Man is Lord of the Sabbath" (Mt 12:8).

Carpe Deum.

I am hungry, oh so hungry today. I am a tired mama, a worn-out teacher, a burnt-out writer, a weary wife.

The bread of the presence, offered right outside my window in a three-dimensional intensity more real than the world it illuminates. In the bright eyes of my children fixed upon me, hoping. In the silence before my *yes.*

There is a difference between demanding immediate satisfaction and being open to fulfillment untethered by the past or the future. There is a difference between approaching time as a complete and separate entity, rootless and fruitless and enclosed in and of itself, and understanding it as a precious link within eternity in which all we do and think and believe runs deep and far and wide. The latter view does not bind us to gravity. In fact, it is the only view that sets us unboundingly free.

When I grow up, I mean way, way up, I hope to be a wise old woman of God. Someone who has learned not merely to seize the day but to seize the Lord. Thomas Traherne, the seventeenth-century poet and religious writer, noted: "We do not ignore maturity. Maturity consists in *not* losing the past while fully living in the present with a prudent awareness of the possibilities of the future."[3] The modernist poet T. S. Eliot, who experienced a conversion to Christianity, similarly speaks of the "pastness of the past" that only the present can hold.

It is how we bring our past, our present, and the promise of our future before God, I think, that makes us wise, that helps us in our pursuit of righteousness. Spiritual maturity can be cultivated by age, by a life steeped in faith; but the two—age and wisdom—of course are not necessarily linked. One can be very old and very foolish. Just as one can be relatively young and yet surprisingly wise. The prophets lived with such intimate dynamics in the chronology of the Spirit. Our conscious recognition of the eternal within the temporal, and being able to act in regard to that ever-present holiness, seems to me our greatest, most innate dignity, so graciously restored.

Yes, gather the rosebuds, to the glory of God. He will weave each one into "a garland to grace your head and present you" (Prov 4:9), so that you may remain in his presence forever. Replace *carpe diem* with *carpe Deum* and you move away from the ledge of self-absorption, from the temptation of falling into spiritual immaturity, epitomized by so many things in the sinful preference of self, but especially by the self-serving pleasure principle. In subtle contrast, *carpe Deum* grasps at God. It seeks righteousness. It touches the robe. It holds onto the Lord and refuses to let go.

Righteousness: such a towering, imposing word. And yet, because Abraham simply believed God's promise, the Lord credited it to him as "righteousness" (Gen 15:6). And so, personally, the best definition I have arrived at in my own spiritual quest for righteousness is *taking God seriously.* Taking him, literally, at his word. Seizing him and holding on. And thus choosing to be in his presence, to seek his presence, with all I am at the human moments when I am capable. For an academic and a believer, the idea poses an entirely different kind of "tenure."

This is the capturing of a vision that turns everything around— not that we become more "successful" in the eyes of the world, for instance, but that we begin to perceive success differently. Is our reply to having been chosen by God to choose to be in his presence as well? And in the choice to love? "Because we love, God is present." Thomas Merton speaks the pulse of the world undivided, of what erases the separation we have ourselves imposed.[4] But loving seizes more than the moment; it seizes God in and through and because of the moment. It then extends this capture to enrapturing others. Biblical love is quite the list: just because it is unconditional does not mean it is not complicated, or easy. The popular verses from 1 Corinthians (13:4-8) often get quoted in the culture at large, and yet the definition of love they present is anything but clichéd.

To even approach a shadow of real loving, as God perfectly loves, takes spiritual discipline in us. We who have fallen away from this first love must labor back through an aging that takes eternity into account with time. This process grows into peace with the past so that it may laugh at the future, so that the heart and mind and soul that loves God first overflows that love to others, and then, only then, can open into the full realization and actualization of deep joy.

Replace the *I* of *diem* with the *U* of others—of God and of people outside of oneself—and you have the old spelling trick again, the sleight-of-hand that reveals the shift in soul. One letter, one small change, and a new way of seeing appears that, again, makes all the difference in the world.

I often forget the *U*—in my doubt, or distractedness, or self-sufficiency, or, at the most pressing times, agony. But then the love of others around me reminds. On many occasions I resonate with Anne Lamott's desire for the presence of God to be immediate and clear and comprehensible:

> God: I wish you could have some permanence, a guarantee or two, the unconditional love we all long for. "It would be such *skin* off your nose?" I demand of God. I never get an answer. But in the meantime I have learned that most of the time, all you have is the moment, and the imperfect love of people.[5]

And so, thinking back on how my mom loved us, and how God loves, and the great chain of love that universally travels through particulars and poetry and prayer, I say yes and eat of the bread of the presence.

The children squeal with delight, toppling out of the kitchen nook in a mad rush to get ready for the beach. Even in the ensuing chaos, I take the time to make myself a real lunch, not my usual scavenger fare left over from the kids' plates. Then I pack the stroller to overflowing and the kids pile on top. We look like the Clampetts from *Beverly Hillbillies* as we pull out all weeble-wobbly from our driveway. Every muscle clenches as I maneuver down the old sidewalk a mound that could rival that of my laundry, but this consisting, more happily, of sand toys, beach blanket, towels, snacks, drinks and kids, all balanced precariously on relatively tiny wheels. The children are jubilant, their glee mirrored in the seagulls reeling above us in that oh so perfect sky. We pull up in front of the beach snack bar, where I stretch out my aching arms. Then I take a few crumpled bills from my pocket for ice cream, and we sit together on top of the picnic table, scanning the horizon for leaping dolphins, chins dripping with double-flavored bliss.

In Communion, when we take the body and blood of Christ in the bread and wine, we do so, as Jesus asks, "in remembrance of me" (1 Cor 11:24). In *carpe Deum*, I like to think the remembering comes with ice cream, too.

A motley crew, we arrive at the edge of the surf, find the best sandy spot and plunk our things down with gusto. I set the stroller against the seawall and unpack all our beach paraphernalia: blanket, balls, buckets, bags. The cornucopia spills out around us, supplies for a sunny day. The kids spill out, too, racing from the stroller out toward the sea, with all the magnetic pull of baby turtles fresh from broken eggshells.

Alone now, I remain in a small circle of relative quiet.

Well, here I am, I think proudly to myself, *practicing "retreat."* Yes, my children are still in tow, but I had taken one small step for harried womankind: I had packed a lunch lovingly prepared *just for me.*

After a few deep breaths of fresh sea air, I seize my moment of opportunity. Giddy with the excitement of discovering tiny sea crabs, the children throw themselves into beach bliss, oblivious to my presence. As they fill buckets with their finds, I reason that they will be far too preoccupied for the usual stream of endless requests (which tend to escalate the moment I sit down). No one is bickering, either, or hitting the other one with a beach shovel—an added boon.

So I tentatively—a habit cultivated by most mothers surrounded by their young—turn toward my lunch. I am hungry ... oh so hungry ... and I long ... oh so long ... to eat my food slowly, without interruption. To taste and chew every bite. Such a luxury at this season in my life! My sister, with her usual flair, once compared being a mother to being the runt of the litter: "Whenever you do get a chance to eat, you gulp it down because you don't know when your next chance will be." A friend of mine, while nursing her third child and taking care of two toddlers at home, similarly lamented: "It seems so ludicrously unfair. Here your body is, a nourishment machine for others—physically and emotionally—and yet you yourself subsist on leftover teething biscuits and cold bits of macaroni and cheese. At best, you might have a day when you can graze, but you don't even have the advantage of chewing your cud."

I have such poetic friends.

Another mom I know shrugged as she picked goldfish crackers off her kitchen floor and popped them into her mouth. "Hey," she spoke to my look, "it's not like they are *that* stale."

"Oh, I'm not offended," I replied, merely clarifying, "except that you didn't share."

"Finders keepers." She grinned back.

"I wondered what the shelf life, or perhaps I should say, floor life, is in your house?" I asked her as she went to get her broom.

"Four, maybe eight hours," she replied, "depending on the perishable factor. I try to sweep before Mark [her husband] gets home. You?"

"Until company is due over," I answered.

"Is that often?" she looked sympathetic.

"No." I stooped down to pick up a handful of partly crushed goldfish, too. They looked good after all, and as always, I was hungry. "I end up delaying because my house is such a mess."

We laughed together.

Here, now, on the beach, the wind lovingly caresses my face. The atmosphere is at the perfect temperature: not a trace of chill, nor a touch of humidity. Within a safe distance, the children have set their prisoners free. Discombobulated crabs scuttle out of upturned pails, madly scrambling for sandy cover. The children squeal and race into ankle-deep water, tossing each other Frisbees and beach balls. After a while, they gather around the common goal of building a mammoth sandcastle in the retreating tide.

I look down at the Tupperware unpacked beside me. The suggestion of a rainbowed meal beckons me through the murky plastic. Green lettuce, red tomatoes, orange peppers, black olives, bite-size amounts of fresh feta cheese—as soft and white as the breast of a woman in an Elizabethan sonnet. All topped with my friend's absolutely to-die-for secret-recipe balsamic dressing. Oh yes. And pine nuts. One handful from the local organic and gourmet grocery store costs as much as my gallon of milk from Costco—this shop is not my usual stop, but my self-indulgent one.

I continue to gaze at the container cradling such a masterpiece of a salad lovingly prepared for me, by me. An act not often completed, a gesture too rarely made. A fiesta of the senses! Fresh and vibrant and full of texture and taste.

I glance up at the children. Yes, everyone is still very busy, still very happy. Here's my chance—before they see me eating. Especially before they see me eating something I have not packed for them. Before they interrupt my mortal needs—eating and sleeping—in their assumption of my immortality. One day, I know, I will miss their childhood supposition; for now, however, I am just very, very hungry.

The anticipation is part of the treat.

My napkin and my plastic fork sit ready on my lap. The gulls swoop and chuckle overhead. I reach over and pick up the meal—not from the sticky floor of chance, but from the deliberate self-care of preparation. I hold it for a few moments, stroking the suctioned lid lovingly. I cradle it in my palms, like an offering—to myself.

I sigh.

My mouth waters. I can imagine myself tasting, chewing, rolling flavors around on my tongue . . . taking one savory bite at a time as the children play, blissfully unaware of my bliss. Today, at least for a few moments swathed in such seamless blue of sea and sky, I am not the runt.

With all the breathless reverence of an artist restoring a classic painting, or an archaeologist discovering a treasure, I peel back the airlock lid. The container kisses open. The salad smiles up at me—all tossed perfection, wearing its crown of cheese and all pine nut bejeweled.

Suddenly, out of the corner of my eye, I catch a blur of orange streaking across blue. Moments later something lands next to me with a heavy thud.

KERPLUNK.

Sand sprays everywhere, stinging my arms and cheeks.

One of the kids has tossed a basketball in my direction. A *basketball?!* I find myself wondering, *Just who brings a basketball to the beach?*

Without looking in their direction, however, I know which child is responsible. One of my sons is all about baseballs; his twin, basketballs. I should have remembered that there is always at least one of each smuggled along on any outing. This time, I realize when I crane my neck around, the culprit had been tucked in the bottom canopy of our double stroller.

Balls—the bane of my feminine existence.

Phew, that was close! I breathe a sigh of relief. *But it didn't land in my salad! The ball didn't land in my salad!* I rejoice silently. I call out an admonition anyway, in my best irritated, this-is-serious mom voice.

"Sorry Mama," the guilty twin responds sheepishly. "An accident! No mean to . . ." I have to admit, such gravity in a baby voice owns a disarming effect.

"Oh, don't worry honey," I sing out, feeling generous with the salad still intact on my lap. "Just don't do it again, okay? You know the rules—no tackling, or throwing objects, without warning." With twin boys in my house, I constantly feel like I'm reliving the Super Bowl commercial where Tim Tebow takes down his mom. I think this is how boys show love. Sweet, even if it does require body padding and rehabilitation.

The kids shout their agreement and go back to playing. They have caught more crabs and are dotting their sloped sandcastle with them, although the walls constantly crumble with the crabs' repeated attempts to escape. Unfazed by their castle's crustacean erosion, the children take turns pushing the basketball through the wet mud, trying to carve out a moat.

Moved into action by the close call, I pick up my fork and greedily stuff in a huge bite. I shudder in anticipation of the love affair between my tongue and the soft, salty feta. My mouth too full to speak, I think a quick grace, adding *God bless the Greeks!* But instead of velvet topped with nutty crunch and fresh herb, something grainy coats my tongue. My teeth immediately grind little bits of a hard substance. I spit out what I can. I wipe the inside of my cheeks with my napkin. I swirl water and gargle, but I still can't get all the grit out. I look down at the ever so lovingly prepared lunch in my lap.

Sand!

Sand lies sprinkled like brown sugar over the entire salad, even filtering down between the lettuce leaves. A few small damp lumps rest triumphantly on top, nestled amidst the pine nuts.

I blink in disbelief.

I try seeing if any of it is salvageable. But no. Grains splattered from the basketball have managed to get into every nook and cranny of my culinary work of art. When I lift a section with my fork, the bottom of the bowl glitters back at me like a fossil. My perfect salad is now perfectly peppered by small particles of inedible erosion. The effect gives an entirely new meaning to the phrase "Santa Barbara salad."

My heart sinks with my stomach. Deflated, I can't help but think of Emily Dickinson's maxim: "When I try to organize, my little Force explodes."[6]

Tired from pushing the basketball through heavy mud, the kids saunter over in search of snacks.

"What's for lunch, Mom?" my daughter asks. Then, eyeing my discarded salad, she adds, "Why aren't you eating your salad?"

"It has sand in it," I say flatly.

"Why'd you do that?" my son who threw the ball admonishes, all guilelessness.

I ignore him and unpack their lunch bag. I wipe little hands, then distribute juice boxes, sliced apples, cheese sticks in the shapes of animals. My daughter eats with meticulousness while my sons scarf down their food, oblivious to the additional sand in which they still manage to coat everything. I reason that some sand probably can't hurt the digestion, maybe even promote it. It is roughage, after all.

The boys gulp and run. My daughter stretches out her towel next to me and lies down.

"I'm sorry about your salad." She pats my hand with sophisticated just-turned-five-year-old sensitivity.

"Thanks." I give her a weak smile.

"Here, have some of my goldfish." She dumps her handful of crackers beside me on the blanket made so sandy by the lunch break as to almost be an extension of the beach. I marvel for a moment at the countless seemingly futile acts required by mothering. Why *do* I keep trying?

"Thanks," I say again. She stretches her legs out from her Little Mermaid bathing suit. I study them: small limbs still reminiscent of their toddler sweetness but hinting at womanly shapeliness now. Oh, where has the time gone? The tide has moved quite far out now.

"You can have the rest!" she laughs, as she abruptly jumps up and runs to join her brothers. I watch her girl-woman legs pump fast across the beach. "Remember to say grace!" she calls over her shoulder.

❊

All of a sudden, without warning, an enormous pewter arch breaks the cerulean surface of the sea.

A gray whale!

And then, as if that were not enough, a *second* whale rolls upward just behind the first. Two gray whales now ascend and descend in perfectly spaced synchronicity like a couple dancing atop a watery mirror.

I jump to my feet, yelling to the children to *look!*

We stand together, along with a few other onlookers on this weekday off-season afternoon at the beach, riveted as these great creatures loom out of the gentle swells. I marvel at their unhurried migration, at the glistening smoothness of their skin highlighted only further by the pockmarks of parasites. What scarred beauty!

We jolt at the explosion from their blowholes as they pass. The children clap and beg the whales to do it again.

"*Carpe Deum!*" I breathe aloud.

My daughter taps my arm.

"Yes, honey?"

She looks at me with the air of correction she usually reserves for the boys, though I have been receiving tastes of it more often lately. "It's not a carp, mom. It's a *whale.*"

Before I can respond, my one son tugs at my wrap urgently. "What is it?" I bend down and ask.

"Is Jonah in there?" he almost whispers. His face remains turned on the whale in awe.

"Not this minute," I reply. "But at one point, maybe in a whale much like it."

I love the four-chaptered book of Jonah. I guess it could be considered to have become cultural cliché, too. After all, the story translates easily to children, and the visuals lend themselves to a graspable cult classic. But again, I see how the gift of the present calls for the unwrapping of clichés, the unraveling of them back to what makes them so susceptible to repeated conjuring. When I peel back the

Sunday school veneer, I see how I cherish the story of Jonah because it is such a human story, such a relatable tale.

I know I often feel like Jonah—called to witness to God, to be obedient, but instead running futilely in the other direction because I either do not feel like doing it or it's not in perfect accordance with my preferences and judgments. On some level I crave a miracle to be convinced, to be jolted into action. Tellingly, when faced with a demand for a miracle from the Pharisees and teachers of the law, Jesus answers with the comparison made to the Old Testament prophet: "For as Jonah was three days and three nights in the belly of a huge fish, so the Son of Man will be three days and three nights in the heart of the earth" (Mt 12:40).

At its core, I think, Jonah offers a story about how incapable we are of being God, and yet how grouchy we are that we are not.

And it is a story about *fear.*

As a result, I find the story of Jonah hilariously funny but somewhat discomfiting, too. Perhaps partly because I identify a little too closely with Jonah's fears, inadequacies and hesitations, and partly because I sympathize with the absurdity of trying to outrun (or ignore) God. Moreover, the ironies—and the great sense of humor—are not lost on me when I think of Jonah, in his reluctance to follow God, being consumed and transformed by a large fish when I later read Jesus calling his disciples to follow him and become fishers of people. Literally (for such an often hard-to-take-literally tale), only by entering the guts of the future sign of discipleship does Jonah gain his own guts. He thereby becomes the ultimate Old Testament fisher of people: the one who literally inhabited a fish until he could face participating in saving a nation.

Often in my life, and especially now as I stood on this lone beach, Jonah speaks to me from within the whale. The hesitant prophet who ran from God's request that he witness to a lost city. The man who slept his life away before being shaken awake by storms and swallowed by a great fish. The man who cried out from the deep to God, the man who loved God and yet dared to be angry with him.

And if I were pushed to admit, I also find the story of Jonah circumstantially compelling. The entire thing, though it can sound crazy if you talk about it in broad daylight on the street corner with an unbelieving friend, ultimately does not seem implausible to me. Swallowed by a whale? Well, why not? Put another way, it offers the easy-to-dismiss-as-crazy kind of story that Madeleine L'Engle claims you must take seriously "because it's truth, not fact, and you have to take truth seriously even when it expands beyond the facts."[7]

But the "scientific" facts are intriguing, too. At up to 175 tons, the blue whale is the largest mammal alive today, and perhaps the largest mammal to have ever lived. Certainly this is a creature capable of swallowing not simply one man whole, but legions. And once you were inside one of these mammoth creatures, it wouldn't be impossible, I would guess, to survive within strategic air pockets or extra space. We now know that exposure to the whale's acidic digestive juices most likely would have bleached Jonah white, from head to toe. Once released and teaching God's truth to Nineveh, would such "radiance" have been akin to the angels'? Would it have helped capture his audience's attention? My thoughts wander to my albino anesthesiologist during the boys' birth: the one who played such an important role in saving our lives . . . I hear his voice reply to fear with miracle: *"See?"*

Practicing *carpe Deum* causes me to ponder: just who could possibly author all of this? Certainly not me—again and again I am forced to admit: I have not the imagination for it all. During my emergency surgery in which my pain medication didn't take, when I finally could speak, my voice came out as a whisper. Although I was shouting within my own head, I realized I was barely audible amidst the cacophony of the frenetic operating room. No one seemed to hear me. The experience was akin to being caught in a nightmare. Or a Metallica video. (The same thing for some.) Blue whales produce vocalizations at volumes in excess of 180 decibels, earning them the title of the loudest animal on the planet. They make a type of "music" very distinct to their race, consisting of four notes. So they are not only the biggest animal, but the loudest. And if you were ever stuck inside one, you would be immersed in "surround sound" evocative of four in a watery furnace.

Could anyone have heard Jonah from within, but God?

Can anyone truly hear any of us from within, but God?

❁

I look down at my inquisitive twin, the one at whose earnest "theological" questions we often smile. The one whose life I almost lost, along with mine. The one who, once he did emerge, was lifted up, triumphant and knowing, stretching out in praise of his own birth. The same being now sea-barnacled to my leg. I stroke his sun-streaked hair. His siblings eventually lose interest in the whales and run back off to the sand dunes with buckets and shovels. But he remains, blond, tanned and strong, like a little Viking next to me on the sand, his gaze fixed on the sea, rapt in contemplation of the prophet-gulping mammal rising and falling before us.

Grace is no nibbler. It swallows and carries us whole.

Often, it takes us where we don't want to go, only to help us realize that's exactly where we needed to be. And that there, our wants are filled. Diana's words echo around me, soft undertones in the crashing of the waves: *It's okay to retreat, Caro. God knows where to find us.*

❋

In the wake of the whales' receding, I watch the children glee over their search for more tidal treasures. Triumphant, my daughter holds up a seashell shaped like a unicorn's horn in one hand, in the other a few sand dollars, some still intact. Her face glows with joy. The boys gather around big sis in admiration.

Eventually they approach me with their treasures held out like peace offerings from the sea to appease what they fear still might be an irritated mama goddess. The children gasp when I crack open one of the sand dollars to reveal the little "doves" inside, and gasp again when I tell them about the legend of the sand dollar, or how these little doves spill out to spread the gospel throughout the world. We pass the sand dollar pieces around for each to inspect. Then my boy who threw the notorious basketball holds out all the little doves to me in a sandy palm.

"These are for you, babe," he says with serious sincerity, using his father's pet name for me.

The tide has shifted, and their shadows fall longer now on the rippled exposure of shore. The waves have grown white-capped in the distance, pounding harder and higher now on a strip of bare rocks. The crashing sound carries on the wind. It is getting harder to hear the children around me. I sit muffled in sea-sound, sad that soon it will be time to head home but grateful for this moment of suspension in the peace of such noisy holy:

> The seas have lifted up, LORD,
>> the seas have lifted up their voice;
>> the seas have lifted up their pounding waves.
> Mightier than the thunder of the great waters,
>> mightier than the breakers of the sea—
> the LORD on high is mighty. (Ps 93:3-4)

My stomach grumbles along with the surf, so I look around me. All that is left are the sandy remnants of my daughter's offered snack. I recall her words, tinkling out of her with the innocent truth of childsong: "Remember to say grace."

Thinking of U-turn friends and sand dollars and whales, I do say grace. I actually speak the words, rather than just think them, this time. Grits of sand still disturb my mouth as I say my prayer. The sensation reminds me of how an oyster makes a pearl—how layers of nacre grow upon a single grain of sand, and then how irritation leads to the formation of the precious, within the protective, proactive layering of God.

How funny life is, this seaside salad. And how strangely luminous these pearls of our souls are, with their growth from irritation to rainbow sheen. I add a final request as I lift my head and open my eyes to the almost-too-beautiful-to-take vista: *Lord, forgive me for my grating expectations. Help me seize you, help me hold on to you instead, only.*

Then I pick up the gritty goldfish from the floor of the earth and eat.

7

Exclamation Marks in the Sky!

Then felt I, like some watcher of the skies . . .

JOHN KEATS

*T*hose who have abandoned themselves to God always lead mysterious lives and receive from him exceptional and miraculous gifts by means of the most ordinary, natural and chance experiences in which there appears to be nothing unusual."[1] So writes Jean-Pierre de Caussade in *The Sacrament of the Present Moment*, and so true it is. Once I started practicing *carpe Deum* with attentiveness and, eventually, gusto, I began to see God's hand in everything around me, and at work in my life in particular.

As I sought to develop the art of attentiveness in my own life, it dawned on me how this requires *lectio*, or, as Kathleen Norris identifies the Benedictine tradition of meditating upon Scripture, "holy reading" at its best. How we learn to truly *listen* to Scripture as we read it can also be applied to how we pay attention to God's presence in the writing of our lives.

Ken Gire identifies "three habits of the heart that nurture a re-
flective life": reading the moment, reflecting on the moment and
responding to the moment. As Gire explains so well, "These habits
can be applied to a passage of Scripture, a photograph, a person on
the street, an advertisement in a magazine, a movie, something in
nature, whatever we can see or hear or in some way experience." Gire
points out that the Bible is "full of people who cultivate these habits,
sensitive not only to the Word of God but to what they saw of Him
in nature, in history, and in the circumstances of their lives."[2]

Put another way, as Yogi Berra said, "You can see a lot by looking."
Or, by looking again.

Early one morning toward the end of my sabbatical year in Santa
Barbara, I took a walk around faculty housing on Westmont Circle.
This is a pleasant circular drive that rounds behind the college
campus on which a small community of moderate homes had been
built to help affordably house faculty in an otherwise astronomically
priced area of California.

I had just spent a rare night away from my young family at
Tabitha's extra apartment nearby. I was taking baby steps in practicing "retreat" while also benefiting from the restoration of U-turn
friends. My husband in particular was supportive of my getting a full
night of uninterrupted sleep followed by a full day of uninterrupted
writing. In my home, my children are constant visitors from Porlock;
I had grown as used to my thoughts vanishing in my waking hours
from countless demands as I had grown accustomed to my dreams
dissipating during my short but disruption-riddled sleep.

To clear my head before I returned to my writing, I decided to
take a brisk walk around the neighborhood. I am an ambulatory

thinker: I find walking conducive to reflection and to prayer. Just as I crested the top of the hill that morning, I couldn't help but notice a very distinct cloud formation in the shape of a large exclamation mark. The image was unmistakable: a cloud stick sat atop a cloud dot. No other cloud—not a single puff—marked the clean page of sky:

!
o

It was impossible, actually, *not* to notice this celestial exclamation mark. Such a christening of my time alone to be, and to write, I chuckled to myself. I also couldn't help but observe that this punctuation of the heavens sat directly above a specific house in the circle. The sight was so remarkable that although I had no reason to at the time, I made a note of the address.

Later that day, as I rounded the corner on another walk bookending my block of focused writing time, only a diffused gauzy haze whispered where the exclamation had once been. I noticed that the house below appeared empty.

Several months later, after we moved back to Seattle, Westmont College offered me a visiting professorship in its English department. While delighted, we faced the daunting prospect of having to return and find a place to live in one of the most expensive and competitive real estate and rental markets in the world. And then we had to achieve such a find on relatively short notice to boot. Despite all our efforts, nothing turned up.

As we grew increasingly panicked, the image of that heavenly exclamation mark kept coming into my imaginative field of view. I didn't know what it meant, but it buoyed me up somehow. At the very least, it gave me a chuckle again. After all, Kent and I shared a wonderful inside joke about exclamation marks—using them to signify our love for each other, and God's love for us, and the great adventure of living out Christ's love in this world (!). But the image kept haunting me, no matter how hard I tried to shake it out of my head. When I prayed, it often loomed. So I thought of ending my prayers with it, just to give God a chuckle in return.

Eventually, the time had come when we would be moving from our house in Seattle. We had rented it out and were moving to Santa Barbara in good faith, even though despite our best concerted efforts we still didn't have a place of our own lined up down there yet in which to live. The clock kept ticking, however, as it tends to do. Soon the U-Haul truck sat at the curb packed, and the car sagged loaded to the gills, with only five little spots scooped out inside for the passengers. The Great Team Weber Pacific Coast Road Trip was about to start (!).

Desperate for accommodation, we finally took Lisa's generous offer to stay at her small condo while she was traveling. This would buy us a few weeks once we arrived to carry on our frantic search, but hopefully now with better luck from a local base. It was far from ideal, but it would have to do. We would be leaving early the next morning, a Saturday, on a drive from Washington through California with three small children under the age of four in our well-worn minivan encrusted with Cheerios and filled with the nonstop digital music of children's toys: the kind that continues to play in your sleep.

I don't know what made me check my e-mail one final time late that Friday afternoon. I certainly didn't expect to see anything there. The time was ten minutes to five; certainly any rental agents or campus contacts had gone home for the weekend. There hadn't been much in terms of leads the last few weeks anyway. My thought was to do one last halfhearted check before hitting the auto reply and packing up my computer for the trip.

But then I saw it. I blinked and cleared my eyes to make sure. But yes, I had indeed seen it: a note from the Westmont College coordinator of faculty housing. She wrote to say that a faculty house had come available, and would we be interested in renting it? A house with enough rooms for all the kids and for a room of my own in which to write. A house in a fantastic tight-knit community of believers with lots of other children and a park nearby. A house from which I could walk to work (a dream with only one older car and varying schedules). A house that came at an extremely fair subsidized faculty rate. For us, a dream house.

I just about fainted but pulled it together to call her right then and there at the number she gave in her electronic signature, praying the entire time that I would still catch her to confirm the acceptance of such an offer. She picked up on the first ring, her voice immediately kind. The house, she informed me, sat at the top of the faculty housing circle. There would even be a small glimpse of the ocean from the hill behind, she happily told me. While I would have been delighted with anything with a roof and four walls, I blurted out, "It will be perfect!"

"While I can assure you it's a very nice house," she said as we wrapped up our conversation, "are you sure you aren't nervous about moving into a house sight unseen?"

"No, not at all," I assured her, and could barely keep from laughing into the receiver. "This is one big hunk of manna, an exclamation mark fallen from the sky!"

"Okay, then," she chuckled back, "I'll send you the details and the rental agreement in an attachment here shortly.

"Godspeed," she added warmly. I thanked her again as I hung up. I didn't need to look at the address; I already knew which faculty house it was.

When we finally pulled into its driveway over a week later, Tabitha and her family had decorated the front porch with balloons and streamers, pictures crayoned by the kids, and a huge finger-painted banner that read:

Welcome Home Webers

Followed, of course, by

!

When you arrive at Westmont College through the formal entrance, you end up on a circular drive draped in trees in front of the glorious Kerrwood Hall. Built in 1929 as the private estate residence, after its donation to the college it has since served as the primary administrative building. Much of its original charm has been kept intact, a delight of Mediterranean architecture mingled with rooms paneled in hand-adzed wood, a patio with an imported Italian fountain (whose effect is—*ah molto bella!*—very Italian indeed) and formal terraced gardens. The campus backs onto mountains and looks out over the sea.

One of the first things to meet my eye outside Kerrwood, though it's tucked amidst the roses in a peripheral garden, was a small but seemly statue of a woman. She gracefully lifts a jug at the well. The figure evokes two women from the Bible who served at wells: Rebecca of the Old Testament, who comes to marry Isaac according to Abraham's prophecy in Genesis 24:14, and in the New Testament, the Samaritan woman with whom Jesus speaks at the well from John 4:1-42. Rebecca draws water from the well and satiates thirst of not only Abraham's loyal servant Eliezer but all of his camels as well. Her actions reveal her generosity and kindness, and thus her suitability for joining Abraham's family. Rebecca is most likely the image intended for a statue commemorating the heritage of a Christian college, I thought. The Samaritan woman at the well, however, demonstrates God's giving, in turn, of "living water," or everlasting life, to those who drink from his goodness—or, we could say here, tongue in cheek, his *wellness* (perhaps I've lived on the West Coast too long to avoid such a phrase). Only later, yet again, would I begin to see the significance of many of the details of this latter story to my own.

Like the statue heralding its gates, in having come to Westmont I felt like that woman at the well of living water. Until I arrived there, I hadn't realized how parched I had become. Serving as a visiting professor at a vibrant Christian college offered me professional reprieve from the pressures of a hitherto extremely secular career path. But I also hadn't understood how much my personal as well as professional reservoir needed to be filled. The institution inspired me with its dynamic teaching and meaningful scholarship, while it also modeled to us loving families and thoughtful lives given for the glory of God. In many ways my time at Westmont College bolstered and helped birth my conversion story into the world. Like the Samaritan woman, I had arrived as an outsider to this faith, and yet Jesus welcomed me and bid me drink. And now, just when I felt ostracized in other ways, especially as I was beginning to feel the effects of having been so public about my faith, he led me to this place.

And so there I stood, amidst the sweet-smelling roses, someone who like all of us, man or woman, thirsted for a long, deep drink from the true well.

The academic year of teaching at Westmont came to an end all too soon, it seemed. The hum of final exams built up to the excitement of impending graduation ceremonies. It was with bittersweet emotion that I watched the tents being pitched about campus and attended various ceremonies in celebration of the culmination of the students' hard work and achievements.

For teachers, graduation is often a celebratory yet sad time. We are excited and proud on behalf of our students, and yet we grieve to let them go. In loving them into understanding, we have grown to understand just how we love them, too. The end-of-year hugs and plates of refreshments and gatherings in quads mark a bittersweet season. *We will stay and you will go,* we think to ourselves as our fledglings depart from their various discipline nests. *A part of us, we hope, flies with you.*

What a delight and an immense honor it was, then, to be asked to give the faculty speech for our graduating majors in the English department. Especially poignant, I realized with an extra twinge of sadness, as I would be leaving along with them.

I touched the statue of the woman at the well as I waited outside Kerrwood Hall to be picked up for the graduate brunch. In my speech to this very special crop of students, I wished to share how I now knew that everywhere around me, to use Ann Voskamp's phrase, "all was well."[3] I longed for them to be filled, too. To see the exclamation marks in their skies. To believe in, and trust, living the story. To also feel the current rushing around them, and to be vivified by it. To drink and be refreshed by the present, gifting, as it flowed by, fast and deep.

Madeleine L'Engle comments on the "synapses" that happen when she reads of the lives of great faith in Scripture: "I read their stories [voices in the Bible such as Ezekiel, or Daniel, or the apostles] with sublime wonder, with rapturous joy, acknowledging that reality cannot be organized by us human creatures. It can only be lived. Indifference goes along with perfectionism and literalism as a great killer of story, and perhaps indifference is nothing more than a buffer against fear."[4] As Sydney Carter famously set to music in his adaptation of the Shaker hymn "Lord of the Dance," Jesus conquers the fear of death with the very *difference* of his life. For us, too, as Anne Morrow Lindbergh writes, "when the heart is flooded with love there is no room in it for fear, for doubt, for hesitation. And it is this lack of fear that makes for the dance."[5]

Fear of God replaces fear of human beings, and in that distinction exists a world (restored versus fallen) of difference. Recognizing, praising and tapping into this immense power shifts our trudging into dancing.

As Christians, we cannot afford to be indifferent, nor are we allowed to acquiesce to mediocrity. Rather, as Craig Groeschel points out in his book *Weird: Because Normal Isn't Working,* Christians should strive to not be normal, to not settle for the stress, exhaustion, despair, fear and frayed relationships that a world without God upholds as the "norm." As Christians we are anything but "normal," because our God is anything but ordinary.[6]

The result of such faith is not a life of indifference but a life that makes a difference. Because we serve such an extraordinary God, we are called to live *in difference*: "Do not conform to the pattern of this world, but be transformed by the renewing of your mind. Then you will be able to test and approve what God's will is—his good, pleasing and perfect will" (Rom 12:2). Others who do not believe *should* look at us and not only wonder why we are "different" but also be led to crave being in that "difference" too.

We are all punctuating steps in the dance of the story, we are all readers of our skies, learning from burnout, growing in relationship with God and with each other, seeking and being open to the holy in the dailiness of things. We can read our lives, our surroundings, like a text also written by God's hand, sometimes subtle, sometimes not, but always appropriate, and in proportion, and to be witnessed or gathered or digested in his good timing. Along with our wounds and wonder, we each become a "reader of the sky."

For me, and I trust that for you, too, my fellow lover (or lover-to-be in the seeking) of the Word, the way things now "sign" to me as a Christian comes with a heightened responsibility to live more deliberately, with a greater attention paid to the text of my life, and its palimpsest relationship to others. We need only look to the heavens to remember.

> Lord, you give us a sign.
> Give us the grace not to miss
> "your" signs day after day.
> Give us the grace to open our eyes.[7]

Amen.

At the Threshold

*Every moment and every event of every man's life
on earth plants something in his soul.*

Thomas Merton

*W*hen I went up the mountain, I would own a secure career, a community and my certitude.

When I came down from the mountain, I would not.

Something in which I had invested most of my life, which had been a lifelong dream, an overriding passion, was left on the summit. So that when I returned to the lower brush where I had started, having reached the mountaintop, after surveying the sea, I had been changed irrecoverably by the journey.

For some time now, Kent and I had been considering more seriously than ever before a return to my hometown in Canada. I wished to spend more time with my children, with my writing, with my aging parents and unbelieving family. I ached to appease the homesickness that had been gnawing at my soul.

Was it just a simple desire to return to whence I came? When I weighed it, and really prayed about it, the draw seemed so much more than just that. Kent had felt it too, even coming to consider the possibility of taking up our writing and ministry opportunities there separately from me. The Lord, it seemed, had led us both to the same page—always a moment of conviction in marriage, I have found.

I shut the door behind me and bounded down the front steps. To clear my head, or center my heart, or perhaps both, I often begin my walks by reciting poetry I've memorized (at least in my head, if I'm worried about being spotted moving my mouth). It's a habit hard-earned from my graduate school days at Oxford, when I realized that learning by rote allowed one to take the words by their root. By this method, many verses I have cherished over the years have come to be written on my heart, for my taking out and recherishing at a moment's notice, anytime I like. It is well worth the initial effort, for the poetry stays with you forever that way, like an old friend. It is the download that uplifts.

Today, as I start out, I practice "Obedience" with George MacDonald:

I said: "Let me walk in the fields."
He said: "No, walk in the town."
I said: "There are no flowers there."
He said: "No flowers, but a crown."

I said: "But the skies are black;
There is nothing but noise and din."
And He wept as He sent me back—
"There is more," He said; "there is sin."

I said: "I shall miss the light,
And friends will miss me, they say."
He answered: "Choose tonight
If I am to miss you or they."

I pleaded for time to be given.
He said: "Is it hard to decide?
It will not seem so hard in heaven
To have followed the steps of your Guide."

I cast one look at the fields,
Then set my face to the town;
He said, "My child, do you yield?
Will you leave the flowers for the crown?"

Then into His hand went mine;
And into my heart came He;
And I walk in a light divine,
The path I had feared to see.[1]

As I step onto the lowly beginnings of the mountain path, I can see why so many poets enjoyed walking, especially the Romantic nature poets. Walking lends itself to a contemplative rhythm, much as poetry does. I follow the slow curve of the path, noticing how it begins with a subtle serpentine slope. My breathing comes easily in the cool shade of the trail here, heavily draped with vines and bush.

I duck through the arch of thickets, keeping my eye on the path like a dirt trough before me, my feet bending inward from its narrow furrow. *I do not know any other way to be but a teacher,* I lament to myself as I stumble along. My life has been patterned by the academic year for almost as long as I can remember. I only know the poetry of the university. My waking and my sleep have grown shaped by the hum of a campus, the electricity of exams, the ebb and flow of grading and meetings and graduation and commencement.

How else to be?

The hill slants more here, the terrain is rougher. My breath labors with my legs. I round the bend past the lone crooked tree.

Suddenly the world goes vertical; the landscape becomes so
steep I must use my hands to grab at the earth and pull myself up
toward the top of the cliff. The effort is so difficult that it aborts all
thinking. It is not until I reach the very top, practically pulling myself
up over the edge with my fingernails, that I can turn around, stop
and catch my breath as well as my thoughts.

From this height, I feel invincible and yet slightly weak at the
same time: admiration tinged with vertigo. Standing at this precipice,
I think of Jesus in the wilderness and how Satan came to tempt him
(Mt 4:1-11). This precipice marks the threshold where vastness
meets tipping point. It is where the sublime lurks, a *spiritus loci*
where fear edges awe.

This kind of locating causes me to ask myself: *Am I testing? Or am
I trusting?*

Below, estates quilt the countryside, a needlepoint in olive and
eucalyptus, with a fine row of tall palms fringing the far-off beach
with blowing tufts of green. There is not much green in this southern
clime, I notice: not like the green that lushes out thick like emerald
robes in the land where I am from, when it is this warm outside.
Almost unwittingly, I compare things again with my native land. The
winter there can be harrowing, coming with a kiss so cold that you
dare not unfold your own body in response for months. And yet it is
worth waiting for the green.

Here the palette consists more of browns: russets, auburns,
ambers, each shade bronzed by relentless sun. Fields unroll yel-
lowed as parchment. No wonder there exists such a threat of wild-
fires for much of the year here. Evidence of the last fire, only a few
years ago, haunts my perch. Even now, on some days when the wind
blows a certain way, my nostrils cringe at the pungent smell of
charred trees. Their broken bodies remain, blackened and bare,

silhouetted with ghostly indifference against cheery blue sky, like hanged criminals someone long forgot to take down.

But what is lacking in green is made up for in blue. Brilliant blue. A blue at times unspeakable. For beyond the browned countryside, the sea billows out, a sheet of rippling azure that mirrors a postcard sky. I sit down now, feet dangling from loose-earthed edge, mesmerized by the way each wave, from here so small, travels from some unknown center toward the shore.

Where do I belong?

Tabitha always says that the sea accepts us. We hand over who we are when we approach it, and it sweeps in and embraces us unquestioningly. In the sea's pulse I empty the currents of my thoughts, my tensions, my worries. I feel my energy flow to it like a river, a great emptying out, when I take it in.

But then again, the seaside is a liminal place: a single place that is two places at once, for we cannot tell where one begins and another ends. A spot of time and timelessness moving in and out of each other at once, like the tide far, far below my feet.

The liminal place can be the mountaintop, the desert, the seashore (and the shore within the seas, parted), the river's edge—so many places the Bible celebrates as the stages on which human drama unfurls. It is the place where laws are dictated and God reveals his glory, where miracles happen, where a faithful mother's hand pushes a doomed child into the mercy of the water amid the reeds. It offers a heightened forum for spiritual warfare, temptation and the potential of losing or gaining one's self, of stepping through the lens and becoming part of the vision.

At the threshold . . .

Sociologists have come to term all the variables that intersect to make us who we are "social locations." But we have spiritual locations as well. Rooted in the earth, in our creation from the "red earth" of Adam, it is no surprise that our deepest longing—to reconcile with God—branches out into the creation for which we were made and in which we are situated.

As this life season would have it, my backyard happens to be the Pacific Ocean. But the landscape evocative of our soulscape need not be overtly and immediately "sublime." Though not as intoxicatingly awe-inspiring as standing on a precipice surveying vast waves of sand or ocean as far as the eye can see, the connection surges up to meet me within the relatively small circumference of my own backyard. It thrills through birdsong, the peripheral movement of lizards zippering stucco walls, the scents of plants and earth and water, or lack of water. The verdant summers of home in southern Ontario meet with the apparent paradox of dry grass rustling in the same breeze that nods the bushes lush with vibrant flowers in my other home of Santa Barbara.

As the Bible illustrates so well, we are a people of place. And we are God's people. So our place, ultimately, is in him. Kathleen Norris puts it beautifully: "The more I am aware of God's presence in my life, and in the world, the more intimate this relationship becomes, the more I am in awe. And the more I stand in holy fear, the smaller I seem in the face of God's vastness, God's might, God's being. 'The fear of the Lord is the beginning of wisdom' is a simple truth, a truth and a fear I can live with."[2]

Liminal space—living on the threshold where the present meets eternity: indeed a truth and a fear I can live with, here.

My decision on that mountain climb that day to eventually leave my formal associate professor position was not intended as an indictment of Christians in academia. Rather, for me it resulted from nudges from the Holy Spirit into a new and different life season: a time still of teaching, but led first by mothering, and then writing. Someone else, another Christian professor, for instance, might serve as a long-standing teacher, or even as a dean or provost, and that is his or her vocation, or good fit. He or she might witness God's light to others in very strategic ways through that calling. For where we feel joy and fulfillment, we experience affirmation of our calling.

Receiving tenure doesn't diminish or increase the jolt of this joy. I had been granted tenure and, while relieved, found that the joy lay outside the realm of promotion or security. Those were fringe benefits, but the joy arose from the core.

And while I cherished the students' love for literature and for me, I wasn't wholly surprised by it. It's like trusting in miracles and then witnessing one, and being surprised, and yet not surprised, by the magnanimity of God. As I like to put it, "a wonder, and yet no wonder." That's how I often felt at the end of a class: that somehow we had all been loved into a deeper understanding of something holy and relevant for that particular day.

The nudges I was receiving, both positive and negative, were attesting to a shift in the use of these gifts. Kent and I had been thinking that we could do the parenting and the writing from virtually anywhere, so why not Canada?

Tabitha waves at me from the bottom of the drive. We have tried to meet up during our walks, though with two busy households and five young children between us this is not easy to coordinate perfectly or often. We thread arms and I lean into her familiar frame, so slender yet so sustaining. Tabitha is one of those rare people who always insist that you talk first. I have tried to learn this gracious habit from her, but I usually end up short.

In an outpouring of words, which basically starts the moment I see her, I tell her as we walk together into the growing twilight about my desire to return "home"—and about how this is more than a desire. I can't fully explain it, but upon finishing my conversion story, I now feel such an urge to *be there* with it. That is, to share the hope of God's healing and love with a people and a place I had lived among and held so dear before I was a believer, but for whom now I feel an obligation of responsibility—*and* a joyful longing—to return.

Such relocation, however, would involve leaving everything we hold familiar and secure, I also tell her. Of course, she already understands this. I am talking more aloud to myself than even to her, weighing all the variables, speaking all the details.

"You and Kent discussed this extensively, right?" she asks me, her bright eyes set intensely on me. She has the brightest eyes I know. Her daughters now have them, too. *Her poor husband doesn't stand a chance,* I often think to myself with a smile, *in that house full of women with the bright eyes.* And indeed, he doesn't. He loves and serves his bevy of bright-eyed sprites to the moon and back.

Yes, I nod. I tell her where we are. That Kent and I have felt the same nudges together. That while this is a surprising development for us, especially given our long focus on our respective careers, it is also, well, not surprising when we begin to notice how the dust has cleared following the renewed God-dynamite going off in our tidy little lives.

"We decided to take some time and pray about it separately over the last week or so," I explain. "To just be present with the idea of moving there, and all that entails, and to weigh it in our hearts before God individually for a while."

She nods. "And?"

"Well, we set aside tonight to share with each other where we've arrived at, after the kids are in bed. A sort of 'leap of faith' date night, if you will." We both laugh. But then we start to cry. Just a little. Change would mean parting, and parting from dear friends, rare friends, is never easy. We sniffle our way toward the edge of campus, down along the track set high above the ocean. Some of the most beautiful views in the world, I think, especially at sunset, are here.

Her eyes glisten brighter with tears. But we do not need to voice how much we would miss each other. We know that friends in God let friends in God go.

"Your pact doesn't preclude praying it over with other friends, does it?" Tabitha gives me a mischievous smile. Her bright eyes dance hard.

Tabitha always reminds me to pray. While I'm getting better at cultivating the habit, at really beginning to grasp it as a lifeline, it was always a somewhat foreign concept to me as a latecomer to the faith.

Ah, that's right! I have started to realize more and more. *I can pray about it!*

Duh.

Tabitha is one of those prayer-whisperers. One for whom it is second nature, for whom it comes unceasingly. I am inspired and fed by this. It grounds me and lifts me up at the same time. We stay linked, a prayer chain of two, walking the campus track around and around and around again, in prayer. Until we are prayed out. We raise every concern, every variable, every logistic we can think of. We pray for pure hearts, for the honoring of husbands and provision of children. We give thanks and request direction. We hand over confusion and worry and all the trepidation of self. Asking, instead, for the peace to know whence the feather falls.

I notice we keep circling the same lane, without thinking. Yes, in prayer we do have the inside track with God.

The lights flicker on, flooding the athletic field. The crescent moon whitens in darkening sky over the observatory beside us. Like the moon, things swirling inside shift from obscurity to sudden clarity. Tabitha turns and smiles at me as we crest the final hill up toward the houses.

"Well, Caro," she gives me a hug at the top before we go our separate ways, "maybe this will be your homing year?"

My momentous mountainous trek comes to an end. I return from the sublime, enter the mundane. I step into the circle of modest houses, aglow with lights now that evening is spreading. I pass bicycles propped on porches, smudge sidewalk chalk drawings with my footfalls. I push thigh muscles up the final steep incline to our house, yard strewn with toys, forlornly persistent Christmas lights still bobbing along the eave.

The screen door creaks and snaps around me. I make dinner, read stories, bathe little ones, put sleepyheads to bed. I pour some juice in our Pier One wine glasses for a date night effect. Then Kent and I finally collapse on our saggy, popsicle-stained couch.

"Cheers." We clink glasses. Our eyes meet. I touch his cheek. Oh, how I love that dear face. I notice his temples are graying more considerably now. My life partner, my God-avowed companion in all things. Such silvering only renders him dearer.

"I have something to tell you," Kent begins.

"I do, too, sweetheart . . ." I start in as well. But then I stop. Usually I win out when it comes to speaking first. After all, I have more words to use up at the end of the day. Kent tends to listen patiently to all of them. Tonight, however, he seems so serious, so intense. Unusual for him. Yes, he is a firstborn, and my no-hesitation leader. But usually, at the end of a long day he sits back while I chatter away, and then when I've run out of adjectives, adverbs and similes, he relays goodheartedly a funny anecdote about one of the kids, or turns to wit what has frustrated one of us. He spins the sour into sweet, mines the best parts of the day. And usually, in no time at all, he has me laughing so hard I can't breathe.

But tonight is different.

He takes my hand.

"I've been giving it a lot of thought and a lot of prayer . . ." he traces our wedding band with his finger. "And I think we should take some time with your family."

I hold my breath. Uncertain. Unsure. Or am I?

"I think we should move to Canada," he states, quietly but clearly.

I look back at him, wide-eyed.

La folie de Dieu.

Crazy for God. Foolishness for Christ. Mad about our Lord.

Those poor "holy fools" who gave up everything to follow him.

I can hear the soft hooting of owls rippling through the night outside our window. I cannot help but smile at the cosmic chuckling all around us. When I don't say anything, he continues.

"I think we should try all the things that have been in our hearts. I want to love on your family at close range, revisit your hometown, and really live and breathe the gospel among them. I want to focus on our children, and the writing. I think it is a good season to share grandchildren with grandparents, to create memories along with opportunities to serve. I'd want to help you gain some closure with your dad, to find some peace for your mom. You know, especially as they are getting older and frailer . . ."

My eyes start to tear up, in spite of myself. Kent takes my other hand in his.

"Maybe there are lots of ways we could help them," he says gently. "Or just love them," he adds.

I don't know what to say. We are part of that sandwich generation, I know: pressed between the needs of young children and concerns for ailing parents. I think of my walk today, or rather, my climb. This path before us is not easy, either. What vista will meet us upon such efforts as these?

Kent continues, "I believe we can really give this ministry of ours a go, in our home, among our loved ones, through words . . . I'm trying to discern this carefully here, in the small things as well as the large."

I nod slowly. Oh Lord, make me a poor holy fool!

Then he cuts to the chase, in a voice clear and strong, though I notice made endearing by his focused use of his pet name for me: "Babe, we need to ask ourselves: what is the best and highest use of our time, our energy, our resources, before God?"

I remain quiet, still unsure what to say. No, rather there is too much to say. So much that I don't know where to begin. Then I find Kent says it for me. Again.

"I want to really trust, Carolyn. To trust God. With you." He strokes my hair, tucks a loose piece behind my ear. The he takes my hands again, clasping them to his heart: "What if we try *really living* this gift of the present?"

La folie de deux! I find myself slightly altering *Dieu* or "God" to *deux* or "two" in my thoughts. Then I let the grace of my private thoughts extend further: *La folie de deux en Dieu!* The crazy folly of two in God! A small, secret smile curves my lips. The wonderful, beautiful, world-ignoring for kingdom-seeking folly of two? Is this the craziness of marriage? Of a marriage in Christ? The truly, madly, deeply of real love? Kent's voice interrupts my inside joke with God, which is actually so serious as to fill me with levity.

"At least for the year," he suggests, trying to bring some semblance of mundane responsibility to the table. My husband is very good at being crazy for God in a highly admirable pragmatic sort of way.

"This kind of swan dive into the mist is not for the faint of heart. It's bold to be sure," he shrugs. "But it's also us, at least right now! And well timed. The kids are not in school yet. And we can 'do our thing' from anywhere. We can tap what retirement is left and make up the rest as we go. Look on the bright side. You'll finally be able to drop the safety of your salary and benefits and follow me into self-employment." He winks sarcastically, as my heart skips a beat. Mentally I widen my stance to keep from passing out and falling over.

"I know you and your glistening eyes, and I think I can see into your heart," Kent continues. "Is it beating in sync with mine, and the godly nudge we both feel? Campus work, close friends here, idyllic-ville . . . all this may circle back for us at some point. But right now, there are other investments to happily be made."

I nod, gripping his hand tighter.

"As the master said to the Cambridge freshman in *Chariots of Fire,*" Kent grins, "'Seize this chance. Rejoice in it. And let no power or persuasion deter you in your task.'"

I have heard him quote this before, one hand open, one fist gently clenched in sincerity, even as he starts to laugh at his questionable rendition of a Queen's English accent.

I squeeze his hand back. We giggle, a little nervously, but a whole lot more happily, together. I feel the bubbles of Anne Lamott's exquisite observation rising up like air pockets in my soul: "Laughter is carbonated holiness."[3]

We stay up late, hammering out logistics, voicing fears, countering with excitements. But in the end, the love prevails over all of our travails. "'Love suffereth long, and is kind; love envieth not; love vaunteth not itself." Get these ingredients into your life," reminds Henry Drummond. "Then everything that you do is eternal. It is worth doing. It is worth giving time to."[4]

In giving us his Word, "God wrote His own autobiography," declares Dorothy Sayers. How are we to answer his story but with our own?

Living a story.

Was this the implicit result of accepting grace? *Living the gift of the present?*

Together, Kent and I sit on the same page of this living story, convicted and content in collusion on the couch. Bound in our departure from all we held familiar and safe. I smile at this glorious man God has given me, settling my head against his arm. We remain intertwined on the couch until sleep beckons us to bed, where we fall asleep to the gentle owl-song outside calling me home.

Yes, in this gifting of the present, love binds time to the eternal. Love makes worth of all the while.

9

The Dear Hunt

I need not shout my faith. Thrice eloquent
Are quiet trees and the green listening sod;
Hushed are the stars, whose power is never spent;
The hills are mute: yet how they speak of God!

CHARLES HANSON TOWNE

*W*hen Kent and I began sharing our decision to take this leap with faith—to give up secure careers to pursue more writing and family and ministry time in Canada—we received a range of reactions from the "you are crazy!" to the "God bless and God-speed!" The latter usually came from fellow believers who were not surprised at worldly uprooting since we were rooted first in Christ. These folks buoyed us up in prayer and provision. Amidst such optimism, the decision began to seem easy.

And yet, now that we had relocated to Canada and were hobbling into the commitment—well, it wasn't *easy*. The doubts threatened to corrode the dream. Had we made the right decision? What if this was a big mistake after all? What if nothing came of it, and we lost

everything else to boot? Were we crazy for having given up everything to come here? For having so blindly trusted?

While it was lovely to be among my family again, I faced a
pounding surf of worries and dashed expectations that I guess all
family reunions bring. Suddenly, interactions that had been distilled
to short visits over the past many years grew to extended time together, wonderful and yet, at times, uneasy. I hadn't expected my
parents to be ailing so obviously now, nor the hidden hostility
toward our faith from others we held dear.

Due to unforeseen circumstances upon our arrival, we got jostled
from place to place, unpacking and repacking and unpacking again,
before we were finally brought, travel-tossed and resource-drained,
to the reprieve of a fortunate rental find. Health care and immi-
gration costs in a new country accumulated. The guy who sold us a
family van ditched town and left us with a lemon. Writing didn't
seem to be the way to cover the rent. Kent's clientele had been se-
verely pruned with our relocation, and now he couldn't be paid at all
until his new residency was processed. With three preschool
children still at home, we had no family able to help, nor friends, nor
funds for a little childcare reprieve. As tag-teaming parents, one of us
was with the children while the other worked. We were committed
to quality time with our children while building our ministry, and
took full responsibility for this choice. It brought us much joy and
we had no regrets, but it also, to use Rudyard Kipling's phrase, "filled
every minute with sixty seconds of long distance run." If I was honest,
I missed making eye contact with my husband, let alone having a
moment to breathe to ourselves. We were trying our best to shimmy
through to our goals before God, to what we felt called to follow. But
we felt stretched thin, and when others surely looked at us and
thought us crazy, it was becoming harder not to wonder the same.

I would try to remember that in serving Christ first, we were promised full recompense at the consummation of all things. I would try to keep perspective by thinking, for instance, of the widow's giving as based on her means, reminding myself that it's hard for each of us in our own way. And then I would try the troubling and yet age-old tactic of comparing my lot to others' and counting my blessings.

Put another way, I struggled with all the fruitless quandaries of keeping perspective when we do not simply hand things over to God and trust in him with all the unfolded beauty of a lily dancing in the field.

When left to my own devices, I tend more toward petty, petulant petunia than lovely, lilting lily.

Frustrated, exhausted and vulnerable, Kent and I began to bicker frequently, usually at my prompting. It wouldn't take long before we found ourselves on the slow slide into the horrible, self-defeating marital game of tit for tat in which all either party wins in the end is the kiss of death.

La folie de deux was turning into Albert Camus's famous phrase *l'enfer c'est les autres* (hell is others). I often had to get out at the end of the day just for a breath; I'm sure Kent felt the same way.

This afternoon the house with its antiquated air-conditioning system feels particularly hot, I notice. Just stepping from the kitchen bubbling with dinner onto the rose-bowered porch gives a degree of immediate relief.

We are giving, I think frustratedly, giving to the max! When is God going to give back?

Like a tetchy child, I roughly pull a blossom from a nearby branch.

"He loves me, he loves me not," I hiss under my breath as I pluck off each petal, one at a time. I study the limp stem in my hand, all that remains, before tossing it away.

La folie de Dieu! The words come out sounding more like vilification than celebration under my breath. Taking another bloom in my hand, my eye travels straight past the burst of pink petals to their spots of rotted brown. I notice the small green leaves are marred by singed holes:

> O Rose, thou art sick.
> The invisible worm
> That flies in the night
> In the howling storm
>
> Has found out thy bed
> Of crimson joy,
> And his dark secret love
> Does thy life destroy.[1]

Bitterness: indeed the "wormwood" of our spirit, the termite that gets under our skin, and then twists and turns and consumes us from within. As Revelation pictures it: "The third angel sounded his trumpet, and a great star, blazing like a torch, fell from the sky on a third of the rivers and on the springs of water—the name of the star is Wormwood. A third of the waters turned bitter, and many people died from the waters that had become bitter" (Rev 8:10-11). This falling of bitterness into our ready selves contaminates our "well," affects the condition of inner, as well as outer, weather, and leaves a bad taste in the mouth of one's soul.

Wormwood: a sure sign I was growing testy in my trusting.

I wasn't prepared for this—or was I? If I had been, the preparation seemed to fall away from me now like shiny but outdated scales, leaving only qualms, cares and uncertainties shivering vulnerably in their place.

❋

On the evenings when I can slip away since we relocated to this jewel of a neighborhood in my southern Ontario hometown, I have stepped out with the sunset along these generously treed streets. In a few moments I enter a nest of meandering roads tucked behind the large campus here, paralleled by main arteries but protected from the hustle and bustle of the city.

I follow the curve of the road to my right, past the Catholic school that had lain dormant all summer but now is alive with echoing soccer kicks, as classes have just begun. A bust of Sir Thomas More blesses through glass as I pass. I cross at the corner, past the old man who mows his lawn every other day. I marvel at the putting green meticulousness of his yard, such a sharp contrast to my own toy-strewn lot, littered with countless Popsicle sticks, wooden remnants of a steamy summer, sweetly devoured.

The hum of the lingering rush-hour traffic from the busy street one block over recedes in my ear as I continue, up and away, turning inward toward the campus, my ankles bending on the growing hill. I pass the third house in, the one with the red trim, and brace myself for the shrill marking of my passing by the cotton ball of a poodle who perpetually popcorns at the screen door. The collie two houses farther offers a more restrained acknowledgment but eyes me suspiciously nonetheless. I give him a nod and step harder into the hill. The spotted cat on the next porch continues bathing, then freezes, sultry eyes on me, with one leg stuck in the air. Then he decides I am not worth the attention and lowers his back paw to separate toes and claws with tongue.

The houses grow increasingly grand along this bend in the road. As I study them, I have to admit it is hard not to covet them. The idea of a home, particularly of "the perfect house," is especially personal for me. In my childhood, we spent hours in the car simply driving through neighborhoods, looking at houses, my mother at the wheel. I didn't realize at the time what craving impelled her heart, given all she was handling as essentially a single and impoverished parent. We would play games, pointing at the houses we liked best, imagining aloud their innards: décor, layout, even the patterns of carpet or china, the make of a piano, the notched wall marking each child's growth over the years. Did stairs lead to a hot attic or cool basement? Did its walls harbor any spinning bookshelves or secret tunnels?

Growing up, the places we lived in were never for us. The very foundation shifted under our feet. I shuddered with recognition when I read Leslie Leyland Field's beautiful memoir *Surviving the Island of Grace*: "Our handiwork was never for ourselves, only for the people we would never know. It was not for our future, only for the present." This type of present, this type of work, "did not feed our souls and hearts." Later, when she has her own family and builds her own home, each room filled to overflowing with their love, she vows, "And this house would not be sold."[2] The difference between these two "presents," one painful and fleeting, the other loving and enduring, was not so much financial stability, as, like Leyland Fields, I eventually came to see, but grace. As the parable truly shows, one is built on the frightening tilt of shifting sand; the other on the security-giving, ageless rock of God—the foundation we find only as we learn to lean into the faith.

Even after I married, our itinerant graduate studies and then careers had called for incessant moving, always in complaintless submission to quirky landlords or questionable architecture, especially as we landed successively in expensive cities where, when it came to the rental market, beggars were far from choosers. When we did finally scrape together enough to purchase a house, the remodeling effort required so much elbow grease that we suffered from locked joints (literally) and a constant feeling of dis-ease: our residence was never for our long-term enjoyment but always for the necessity of a quick-as-possible resale.

Are we always to be so transient? I often lamented. *Always doomed to never quite having a place of our own?* How I longed for a home! A "real" home: a house with character set on green grass, with a white picket fence and a porch swing and a tree overarching it all with eternal loveliness. A place of meaning like the inherited country home in E. M. Forster's *Howards End* that you lived and loved hard in, then passed on to your children to do the same.

Silly? Perhaps. Especially in this day and age when almost no one can claim to have been born in the same house in which they will die. But still: while we can dismiss our longings as trivial, as impractical, that often doesn't make them any less real, or, sadly at times, any less debilitating.

Birch. Blue spruce. Canadian maple. Then the perpetually autumnal Japanese maple, all crimsoned-purple explosion in front of the conservative beige and white house. Then the apple trees, the curb cobbled with their droppings.

The lane. I must remember to look for the lane. I will miss it and walk right past if I do not remember.

I see it. Then I don't. Is that just another driveway? All the driveways look the same, long and path-promising, on this tucked-away crescent. Nothing specific marks the actual lane, only the accustomed countdown of tree varieties. Or apparently nothing else seems to. Until I realize that the street sign is tucked into an over-growth of foliage.

I sigh as I take in each immaculate house, one after the other. As I covet the tire swing dangling from the aged oak, the stepping stones laid lovingly in the garden, even the recycling box at the curb on which the owners have written their surname, in permanent ink.

I sidestep the rotten apples, and turn.

A sheet of bumpy old road opens in front of me, ending in castle.

Well, it resembles a castle.

It's actually one of the campus's oldest colleges. But when my daughter first saw it, she called it a castle. And as children's perceptions tend to do, the description seemed more than apt, and so it stuck.

Children. Another sigh comes forth from deep within. Test upon test has confirmed, without doubt, the doctors say, no more for us. I am grateful for three healthy ones. I count my blessings again, in that bittersweet very human way. Oh, what a bounty there! Beyond my expectations or just deserts, of course. But how I secretly long for at least one more: we are so enjoying the others, and watching them enjoy a new little one would be so wonderful. But the doctors have passed unanimous judgment, and my body has reiterated the sentence.

I walk this quiet country lane, always, with reverence. On the pilgrimage under silvering leaves strung with bursts of Christmas-red cardinals, I pray through my day's worries, my hopes and my pleas. My discontents and my thanksgivings. A gravelly psalter crackling beneath my feet.

I pass the Precious Blood monastery on the left. An unassuming building, what looks to be two stories of postwar brick. No embellishments or gardens. But if you peer into the backyard, visible from the road only to searching eyes, you glimpse a large sculpture of Christ on the cross, mourned by the Virgin Mary and Mary Magdalene. The magnificent effect of the stark white statue is all the greater against the low surrounding fields of whispering yellow-green. How does such a scene shout so loudly and yet call for such silence at the same time?

I continue walking by the monastery's simple windows, weathered mailboxes, ruddy walls—and catch something again astoundingly white from the corner of my eye. I look back. The archangel Michael in marbled majesty startles from the east wall, exquisite and fearsome. Mighty wings outstretched, he hurls himself in passionate descent upon the unsuspecting sojourner. I remember that this is the job particular to angels: to strike the terrible beauty of God into us mortals in the guise of a message. But I do not like to be reminded.

I quicken my pace.

Although I try to pray, the anxieties swirl in my head, distract my heart. I slow down, suddenly out of breath. Not from my physical pace only, I'm sure.

Soon I am at the smooth cement path that will lead to campus. No bicycles or skateboards or rollerblades, reads the sign. In compliance, I set foot to stone and continue the pilgrimage, winding toward the castle, coming to pass under the high relief of the mother and child. I look up at Mary holding the infant Christ. Her features worn from years of exposure to the elements, she holds her child tightly while surveying the horizon. As somewhat of an eroded mother myself, I can relate. But in this she is unlike me: no distraction exists in her pose or her weathered face. Some quality endures, some kind of strange serenity remains. This is no fair-weather woman. That is one of the reasons I find myself at her feet, actually.

This is why I have come to seek the deer.

Throughout the day, the clock ticks, and I tick with it. A ticking bomb. Sometimes I am successful at being calm, at being present. At being attentive to the children, the husband, the paperwork, the household chores, the friends, the family, the many gifts, even in demands, around me. But often I am not. I am harried and hurried. I keep time with adrenaline rather than with affection. I multitask and fret and race and miss: there is a rush in the rush, and in doing so, in dying so, I forget to breathe, the breathing so central to running a race, to giving birth, to inspiring others, to living life itself. This irreverent breathlessness belies my fear of entertaining angels outside visiting hours.

On many evenings of this steamy summer the air has held me close, as though I had been baked inside a loaf of bread. Some evenings it rested soft as a pillow on my cheek, so soft it was, as if every inch of my naked self were wrapped in velvet. I really could touch it, this distinction between me and the rest of the universe drawn by my own skin.

This evening, however, even though the day had been sultry, the air has cooled. The breeze gently billows against me like new cotton sheets. The dusking sky spots with spiraling leaves, heralding autumn.

After dinner, I often leave the sink of dirty dishes and the couch of tired, equally dirty children to make this hunt. Cooking smells in my hair eventually blow away, replaced by the scent of a dying summer. Tonight, the woodsy perfume is so heady in the damp from the previous day's storm that I have to stop not once but many times during my walk just to breathe it in. Surely this will be one of the lingering fragrances to fill our lungs in the restored world?

As I round the far corner of the castle, I catch my breath now for a different reason.

All of sudden, beyond the civility of campus, homes and treed walkways—without warning—the land drops away and a huge bean field stretches out, an outpouring of silvering green, far and wide.

The eye soaks in pure verdure, without a browning leaf or pinking blossom of distraction. I can trace the movement of wind on the crop's otherwise sea-glass-smooth surface, as the leaves ripple gently beneath the other greater sigh happening over mine.

No matter how many times I round this corner, no matter how many times I approach this grassy precipice, I am never prepared for the intake of breath prompted by this view. For my audible, indecorous gasp (fortunately witnesses are rarely around). I am never quite prepared for the vista's unapologetic effect on my soul.

But then there often exists a second gift within the first.

You have to look closely. You have to be still. You have to search the green. But often, they are there.

Deer, in twos or threes, but sometimes I have counted as many as a dozen, come to the field at dusk to graze. They move so slowly and silently that it can be hard to see the deer for the leaves. But if you are quiet yourself and patient, they often emerge from the perimeter more boldly, and before you know it, a small herd is grazing just below your gaze.

This evening, a stag wades deep into the haze resting on a world spun still. At the crack of twigs beneath my footfall, he raises his head, and great antlers spear the darkling air. He, too, listens. The hart at the center of the growing green.

Such sweet surprise! Such discovery of delight!

> Come away, my beloved,
>   and be like a gazelle
> or like a young stag
>   on the spice-laden mountains. (Song 8:14)

Or on an otherwise easy-to-pass field in the midst of a sprawling, busy campus. On the back roads of a mainstream neighborhood in a midsized town. On the short walk of a woman who was running on empty but is now, gradually, being refilled.

I breathe in the birdsong, the sweet smells rich around me. Then I sit down in the thick grass edging the field. As the descending sun fans amber across the field, the enduring words from St. John of the Cross rise up from within: "At the evening of our day, we will be judged by our loving."

It is the loving, not the longing, that matters most.

The pastor at our new home church here often says, "If you can worry, you can pray."[3] I don't know how many times I've returned to this phrase, rolled it over, considered it like a pearl in my palm and tucked it back in my pocket for safekeeping. This is one of those times when I pull it out. I need to keep it on my mental dashboard, a sort of spiritual GPS. I need to wear it like a memento mori about my neck, adorned by irritation morphing into the precious when wrapped in God's hands.

From this gentle slope, I watch the deer and really try to hand over my worries to God. All that is pressing in, I push back out. I give these grains to him, not in some trite effort but in a true desire to lean in and let go all that may seem silly or selfish but is relatively meaningful to me, a chip in my armor in him, and my amour for him.

Specifically, I pray for something I have never actually tried praying for before: I ask with all I am that my embittering desires be lifted from me. I kneel in the grass and ask God to remove everything that is not a desire first and foremost for him.

Pastor Jon identifies an idol as anything that vies to get your attention away from God, and wins. *Anything.* Will I give anything that power and hold over my life?

I was beginning to see that when we live in perpetual breaking of that very first and rudimentary commandment, the whole house of cards falls. And for good reason. God must be the Alpha and Omega of my desire if I am to truly live, or else my desires will consume me and I will die not only the Great Death, but countless little deaths landing like stinging nettles on exposed skin, every hour of every day.

My prayers were not to become an ascetic—not to scourge myself for cravings nor deny myself of pleasures. In fact, quite the opposite: I desired that in longing for God first, and entrusting all my other longings to him, I would be fulfilled by an abundance far greater than I could ever imagine, or wish for, on my own. There exists deep pleasure in coming to a true understanding of the Lord's grace as sufficient. I have had tastes, but I craved a more consistent diet.

❋

I stand up, pick loose a few strands of grass that cling to me. The world still will not let me go.

"The chief riddle that perplexes the common man is that paradox which theologians formulate in the statement that 'God is both immanent and transcendent.'" Dorothy Sayers sums it up well, this presence of God.[4] I know him to be far and near. Vast and intimate. Above me in the farthest galaxy, and within the print on the palm of my hand. Even if I remain for now only at the edge of prayer, at the forefront of the hunt.

As I stretch, raising hands high to purpling sky, I spy one of the old estate houses peeking through the wood. The dirt road below ribbons through the farmland, disappearing and reappearing through the trees. I trace it with my eyes, making out how it finally surfaces in cobblestoned majesty at the manor's front courtyard. If I squint, even at this distance I can discern the original estate's architectural grandeur: walls of pearly gray stone, massive carved wooden doors, copper-capped turrets glinting in the setting sun.

The epiphany flares up with all the astonishment of Pentecostal flame! The words from Scripture speak to me without warning, settling upon me with the astonishingly hushing beauty of the bean field, stilling me with its gaze like the deer:

> Do not let your hearts be troubled. You believe in God; believe also in me. My Father's house has many rooms; if that were not so, would I have told you that I am going there to prepare a place for you? And if I go and prepare a place for you, I will come back and take you to be with me that you also may be where I am. (Jn 14:1-3)

Instead of the usual covetous pang for an earthly home, I suddenly experience deep peace at the promise of my eternal one. I realize, too, that of the casual smattering of Bible verses I did encounter as a child, this has long been my mother's favorite. Growing up, we spent years driving through affluent neighborhoods, faces pressed against the glass, and we took countless walks along rows of beautiful homes. Does she know how deeply her true want is speaking to her, too?

The vision rising up to meet me reminds me that my perfect eternal home exists in God. It is always there, waiting for me to inhabit it, to make it my own. In heaven it will be fully actualized, prepared intimately for me, as it is for each of us. It is ready. It is there. If it were not so, he would have told me. The hunt, the pursuit of this want, lends direction when we set the needle back on him: "You know the way to the place where I am going" (Jn 14:4).

I turn to go: to bathe babies and turn down beds and tuck in bodies—and then, when the children breathe deep in sleep, to work late beside a man who has leaped in love, too. A man God has entrusted to me, who, I am reminded, is worn even more threadbare than I, and so needs this gifting of the present, too.

My step grows light. Bees dance in the goldenrod, which bends as I pass, as heady, as hearty, as I.

On this pilgrimage to the dear.

10

Grumble and Trust

Above all, do not be afraid of this wonderful life,
lived hour by hour and day by day under
the guidance of thy Lord!

HANNAH WHITALL SMITH

A blizzard moves in the evening we discover I am pregnant. We sit in the kitchen, lit within against the darkness outside, stilled in our quiet center like figurines within a swirling snow globe. Shaken, dazzled, wound up with the music at the base of things, we dare not let out our breath until everything settles.

It had been so clearly established that we couldn't have any more children. Following my last round of tests, in fact, the specialist declared that our chances were far slimmer than winning a lottery. We had become resigned to the reality, though I have cherished a secret hope— one of those grace thoughts, I smiled, known only between God and me. I blink through my reflection in the window before me, trying to discern the landscape behind the flurries outside. Wonder, delight, anxiety all mingle together now. *Well, I'd better buy a lottery ticket,* I think.

Kent says my name in that way only he can say it, and I stop putting away dinner dishes and look up, met by four pairs of eyes bright upon my own. The children wiggle with the sense that something big is coming—something small, but significant and worthy of their attention. The biggest pair of eyes shines with a joy that is palpable. In spite of my worrying habit, I feel the joy shimmy down my spine and fill me up, too.

"Babe," he says softly but strongly, "no matter what happens, no one can take away the joy of this moment, or the fact that this life has existed. Both are ours, and, ultimately, both are forever. And I trust there is more where that came from."

I bend my head as he quotes the lines he loves from the prophet, and with which he has so often gifted me: "'For I know the plans I have for you,' declares the LORD, 'plans to prosper you and not to harm you, plans to give you hope and a future'" (Jer 29:11). The tears finally fall.

"Come." He pats my seat at the table. I set down the damp towel along with my resistance to trust and come join the table. The children remain quiet for once, as we hold hands while Dad leads us in prayer. We open our hearts along with the Bible to Psalm 139: "For you created my inmost being; you knit me together in my mother's womb" (v. 13).

"I sure hope he knits us a girl," Victoria says under her breath to me. "We have enough boys around here."

Yes, the present is enough, I laugh inside, cradling evermore in my heart the Word read and the words spoken, the hands clasped in a circle, the life and love here.

Scripture, fellowship and prayer. This trinity used to intimidate me, baffle and even annoy me. It still does at times, even since becoming a believer: sometimes especially so. But oh how this season of trusting, of really trying to trust, has brought their interrelationship into better focus. Though they remain inexplicable in effect and nature to me— offshoots of a God whose ways are ultimately mysterious, too—they have become clearer and dearer. They have become intangible realities, ways of knowing God that I now turn to with all the urgency I would apply to appeasing a physical hunger or thirst.

Scripture, prayer and fellowship show us, again and again, how we live the metaphor into the heart of the very most real. As a literature professor, I have come to admire how God uses even the most skeptical of secular minds to expose the most sacred of truths; nothing lies beyond the glimmer of his salvation, not even cynicism, which I find to be a shocking grace in and of itself. Christians must be responsible, of course, in helping each other believe, and believe wisely. But nothing made by humankind, in thought or word or deed, can tarnish the glory of God.

What is sadder to me than the arguments of atheists that must eventually come up empty, then, is how they settle for the emptiness. God, however, only creates from such voids. Even God-critic and author Milan Kundera, for instance, recognizes that "metaphors are not to be trifled with. A single metaphor can give birth to love."[1] The Word as flesh embodies just that.

I spend the winter cocooned in the secreted knowledge of a new little life budding inside of me. Even extreme nausea and fatigue cannot dull the cherishing of that special season when two are yet one. The months swirl by with the snow, and in my maternal hibernation I taste my growing need for Scripture, for fellowship, for prayer. Expectancy of body encourages just such cravings in the soul, I suspect.

Yes, manna these three have since become to me, especially in the art of *carpe Deum*. Pieces of provision in the midst of my exile, to sustain the turning of my steps back home.

A few months into my pregnancy, prenatal blood screenings indicate a problem with the baby. The numbers relay a high positivity for a birth defect and possibly a congenital heart condition. My doctor talks to me about these numbers, which are "not good, not good at all," and what that means. He refers me to the genetic counselors, who will explain subsequent diagnostic procedures and viable options, including therapeutic abortion. Nurses flutter about me, booking all the follow-up appointments.

I feign composure. I nod and listen. Or try to. But the doctor's subsequent words mumble outside my comprehension, much like when Charlie Brown listens to adults speak in the cartoon. I make eye contact, attempt to focus, but in spite of myself, my eyes keep returning to the "car accident" at the side of my life road. I steal furtive glances at the bolded print, set within a box at the bottom of the test result page:

> **SCREEN TEST: POSITIVE**

When the doctor leaves the room for a few moments, the words loom up and I sink fully into their terror. The anxiety tumbles inside me on high speed. I have brought my three other children to the appointment with me. Thank goodness, they are well behaved (for the moment), preoccupied with crayons and coloring books in a huddle on the examination room floor. It is important to remain calm, to answer their endless questions about the medical supplies around them, the pigeons outside, whether we can ride that cool glass elevator again on the way out.

I check my voice whenever it grows too shrill. To each question I calmly volley back an answer, grateful for the pedestrian stream of chatter. For questions that don't require anything of me.

When the doctor returns after a consultation, a follow-up procedure is recommended, to be done as soon as possible. The results, he assures me, will help determine more precisely what is wrong.

I try to breathe. The children are getting restless. One boy climbs on my lap and starts running a little race car up the side of my face. My pretense at concentration would be comical, if it weren't for the fact that my heart is breaking. I finally succeed in taking a deep breath. The nurses look at me expectantly. I tell them that, for us, abortion is not an option. But that I will go home and discuss things with my husband.

By now the toy race car's wheels are stuck in my hair, and my son is pulling to free the beloved toy with everything he's got. I wince while I mentally record the next genetics appointment. Again, because of the upcoming holiday, there will be more waiting . . .

Like Theseus deep within the labyrinth, I hold on to the golden thread of my husband's words from within that kitchen buried in snow, it seems oh so long ago: "No matter what happens, no one can take away the joy of this moment, or the fact that this life has existed." I twist the yarn around my heart, refusing to let go, trusting it will lead me away from the monsters, out of the winding dark and into the light: "'For I know the plans I have for you,' declares the LORD, 'plans to prosper you and not to harm you, plans to give you hope and a future'" (Jer 29:11). Although no one sees the tears this time as I bend down to pack away toys and test results.

❋

I *do* like food, I think, as I finally put my feet up at the end of a long day and conveniently balance a new bag of Cheetos on my large shelf of a belly burgeoning with child. Ahhhh, orange melt-in-your-mouth bliss! Surely, though white like coriander and honeyed in taste, manna had that fantastic consistency of Cheetos?

Manna.

It was not something with which they were previously familiar. These wandering and wondering people so many years ago, seeking sustenance in the arid terrain and crying out to their God for help, asked what it was when they first saw it.

The word *manna* in Hebrew means "what is it?"

Their response makes me laugh with them, not at them. I would have exclaimed the same thing! And we still don't really "know" what it was, except that God sent this "bread" to appease a grumbling people. The book of Exodus tells us it was similar to frost in appearance and tasted like oil and honey wafers.

Manna, oh manna! A sweet, strange wafer that appeared in the morning but soon melted away. The interesting things I found about manna, as I sat there balancing my Bible beside my crackling Cheetos bag, are that it is *timely* and *in proportion*. No matter how much or how little one collected, it was always the right amount. A provision rained upon the undeserving, that tested their obedience and required their faith, and that could only be collected at a certain time, could only be held for a certain time and could only appear in a certain amount. Anyone who tried to keep some for the next day—that is, anyone who didn't trust in the timely and appropriate provision for the following day—woke to find their hidden stash stinking and crawling with maggots. And yet the double collection allowed for the Sabbath lasted beautifully until morning.

Manna, it would seem then, embodied literally a "one day at a time" provision. In this sense, its presence exacted trust from the Israelites: trust that the Lord would, indeed, provide what they needed in the perfect amount at the perfect time. The conditions surrounding its provision and proportion in this "test" of trust were quite specific. God should have told the ungrateful wretches for whom he had just parted waters to take a hike. Actually, they already were—okay, so perhaps strike them down with lightning or forget them altogether. Let them starve out there. But he didn't. He could have cast stones down on them. But he didn't do that either. Instead, actually, he rained down . . . bread.

Grumble. Grumble. Grumble. That's all the Israelites seemed to do when the Lord was delivering them from Egypt. Poor Moses. Stuck in the midst of that desert with a God who preferred to speak only with him, and a people who blamed the messenger. Thank goodness he had a brother. The Israelites became so disgruntled they eventually began to *prefer* their old life of bondage and suffering at the hands of the Egyptians. "At least we ate well there," they essentially complained. What a miserable, moody, self-pitying group of—people just like me?

I saw, again, from the manna story, as from the Jonah one, how you can't sidestep God. You can't do a sleight-of-hand with him. Faith is an all-or-nothing affair. No stashed power bars when you are required to travel with your pockets empty. *Not even a Cheeto,* I sighed.

Obedience. Even in the face of hunger. Even worse—in the face of appeased hunger but the fear of that hunger's return.

Hunger for food, for fame, for things ill- or well-intentioned—for anything but God.

"To obey is better than sacrifice," Samuel tells the fallen king Saul (1 Sam 15:22).

Faith in a desert.

Trusting in his timing.

Oh these stories of old, do they speak to us today? I look for the gifting of the past in my present. I search for the manna frosting the ground. Is it maggoted now, decayed? Has it dissipated, melted away? I hold prenatal test results in shaky hands, tacked to the world of grumble and trust.

I love words. Words are what I "do." So of course I have grown more and more fascinated as a believer by the dimensions of understanding *word* in relation to God and his Word, as defined by holy Scripture. "The Word" has a rich meaning throughout the Old and New Testaments, where it refers to God's revelation *and* manifestation. For instance, when John describes Christ's second coming, he also assigns him the title "the Word of God" (Rev 19:13). He identifies a deity that is personally present and tangible. Thus, "the 'Word of God' is always 'God with us,' *Immanuel*."[2]

One day as I sat reading, I suddenly became aware of just what a *profound* experience the act of reading itself is. As a relative newcomer to the serious concept of Christianity, I had been struggling with the notion of the Trinity (who doesn't?). No matter how hard I tried, I just couldn't wrap my head around the idea of a three-personed God. Just who was this one-in-three, this Father, Son and Holy Ghost?

No matter how hard I tried, Don McLean's lyrics to "American Pie" kept creeping into my head. I kept imagining three homeless guys on a train bound for the coast. Somehow I couldn't reconcile this with Pentecost, or a manger, or a cross, or infinity. I didn't see that it wasn't about wrapping my head around anything, but about having the Holy Spirit wrap around me.

It continued to freak me out. And not just a little. Trying to grasp the Trinity seemed akin to trying to stare down a psychedelic pattern from the 60s. Whenever I thought of this Father-Son-and-Holy-Ghost thing, I felt like I needed to shake my head until my vision cleared. How could God be all-powerful, all-present, all-good and yet fragmented? I hadn't yet made the connection that it was precisely because God *is* all powerful, all present and all good that he *can be* all three. Rather, for me back then (and sometimes still), they blurred together. They didn't, well, *make sense.* I wanted a God I could catch in my hand, hold in my consciousness. Especially if I was going to put all my trust eggs in this seemingly frail basket. I wanted the one bird to hold: not the two off somewhere in an inexplicably burning bush.

But as I lay reading—quite literally one day on the slanted floor of my tiny English dorm room, with pigeons clucking angrily outside my concrete view—the nature of the Trinity flashed upon my understanding with all the silvered glint of a fast-moving fish in a creek. Too quick to catch, but the sheen proof it is beauty-fully there.

There is the author outside of the story, who writes the story, and sometimes even writes himself into the story. Then there are the characters in the story, autonomous in terms of their actions within the story, and their determined free will (no, I do not think two such concepts must be at odds) holding consequences for themselves and others. Then there is the reader reading the story—me—moving the parts together so they make sense in my own mind and in the process becoming a part of my own life experience. These entities were not random, nor were they separate. They were, actually, amazingly interlinked, and their relationship created meaning as it could be apprehended by me, the reader.

Something "electric" happened in the reading itself. Some transaction between the author and reader. Some type of synapse exchanged between the characters, too (including the narrator), and the reader.

All these dimensions of the text, and then of the metatext, were not exclusive. Nor were they "irrational." But the effect worked so smoothly as to belie the intricacy and potency of the forces at work. Like watching a talented figure skater on ice: medium, skill and surface all become one, and oblivious to the complexity (or at times, with fleeting appreciation for it), we are transported by the movement and the music.

This insight couldn't have struck me harder than if a heavy book had fallen on my head. It was definitely a Newtonian moment for me. *Reading is a trinitarian act,* I realized. It is indicative, like all creative acts, of *A* and *C* connected by that third something, that *tertium aliquid,* as the Romantic thinker Samuel Taylor Coleridge puts it, of the mysterious force in *B.*

As I eventually became a Christian and began to read more in the tradition of Christian thought, I realized that this insight was nothing new, of course. Lewis, Sayers, Vanauken, to name a few—many others had illustrated the tripartite imaginative force according to such an analogy. And though it is not perfect, the analogy does convey the "spirit" (if you will) of God's moving parts among us, and yet also the stillness that comes with knowing he is God.

While other Christian thinkers have confirmed or helpfully elaborated this insight, for me, reading will always carry the fragrance of this very personal epiphany. As I enter text, taking the Word at its word, I am reminded of my intimate brush with *kenosis*—the self-limitation of Christ's divine power at the incarnation—and of how this true omnipresence can, as Roger Pooley explains so well, "translate into a Christian aesthetic."[3] And, I would add, into a beautiful way of being when we believe.

"The Bible is the word of God, and a religious poem by Nietzsche is not," states Dietrich Bonhoeffer. "This is the unsolvable mystery of the revelation of God in hiddenness."[4] Just what is this mysterious effect that condemns or convicts the reader? On this side of heaven, we will never know. But the closest I have come to putting my finger on it, I think, falls in the final words of Frederick Buechner's aptly titled book *Telling the Truth: The Gospel as Tragedy, Comedy and Fairy Tale*:

> Let the preacher tell the truth. Let him make audible the silence of the news of the world with the sound turned off so that in that silence we can hear the tragic truth of the Gospel, which is that the world where God is absent is a dark and echoing emptiness; and the comic truth of the Gospel, which is that it is into the depths of his absence that God makes himself present in such unlikely ways and to such unlikely people that old Sarah and Abraham and maybe when the time comes even Pilate and Job and Lear and Henry Ward Beecher and you and I laugh till the tears run down our cheeks. And finally let him preach this overwhelming of tragedy by comedy, of darkness by light, of the ordinary by the extraordinary, as the tale that is too good not to be true because to dismiss it as untrue is to dismiss along with it that catch of the breath, that beat and lifting of the heart near to or even accompanied by tears, which I believe is the deepest intuition of truth that we have.[5]

Scripture is manna.

Have you ever noticed that when you wash your feet, your entire body feels refreshed? Think of taking a long walk along a dusty road on a hot day, and then dipping your feet into the coolness of a creek—the effect on one part ripples out to the whole.

I am reminded of this when I contemplate the feet washing that takes place at the Last Supper. I marvel at a Lord who would stoop to bathe the lowest part of his servants. There are so many ways to "wash another's feet," so many manifestations of the statement by Jesus to his apostles: "A new command I give you: Love one another. As I have loved you, so you must love one another" (Jn 13:34). Servitude creates fellowship, a love for one another that speaks more loudly than words. And so the next verse in John reads: "By this everyone will know that you are my disciples, if you love one another."

"Praise be to the God and Father of our Lord Jesus Christ, the Father of compassion and the God of all comfort, who comforts us in all our troubles, so that we can comfort those in any trouble with the comfort we ourselves receive from God" (2 Cor 1:3-4). Fellowship offers mutual manna, given by God not only directly to us but also through us to each other, through God. Paul explains, "At the present time your plenty will supply what they need, so that in turn their plenty will supply what you need. The goal is equality, as it is written, 'The one who gathered much did not have too much, and the one who gathered little did not have too little'" (2 Cor 8:14-15).

Interestingly, I find, Paul continues to refer to the manna of the Old Testament in Exodus 16:18. As with tithing, this provision can refer to money but also to so much more. Paul shows how in God's economy, equality is established without politics in this proportion and timing of mutual giving, this "presenting" among those in Christ. The new, never-decaying "bread of the presence" bonds those who eat of the body, who partake of the "present."

Fellowship is manna.

Without having to close my outer eyes, I close my inner ones to the distractions, ingratitudes, busyness, wanderings, uncertainties... And I soak up, take in, all the prayers offered now for me. How much in our lives do we unknowingly owe to someone's prayer for us? Prayer crosses all boundaries. It knows no gender, language, syntax, expectation or delineation. It makes babble coherent. Prayer makes form out of my chaos.

And I pray that these pieces of peace will sustain me, and will sustain others. At times of bad news, what words are there? How do attempts at compassion, at consolation, come up as anything but trite? What manna can possibly fill this hunger? this loss? And yet I present my prayers to God on our behalf anyway. I groan inwardly, for me, for others. Each day we must pick up pieces of God, collect him here and there.

Because of God's love for me, my bowl is never empty. My prayers are never in vain. I remember how I will be filled when I am finally fully in his presence, and I remember God's own bowls before that ultimate altar: bowls filled with incense, which we are told consists of the prayers of the saints (Rev 5:8).

Prayer is fellowship when you can't be there in person. Those who pray for us, indeed, in God, sustain us.

Prayer is manna.

In this stilling, stillness, I consider the indescribable—the mystery—within Scripture, within fellowship, within prayer, and I, too, ask with God's people: *What is this?*

Scripture. Fellowship. Prayer. I recognize I need regular doses of them. Portions of my daily bread.

God is everywhere, the Great I AM. But I am not. And so I can see only the glimmers, the patches—sometimes, the odd time, a great expanse, but often, more often, the crumbs. The little broken bits, like Communion wafers.

But still, I take and eat in remembrance of him, and must trust that even the crumbs from the table are enough to sustain me (Mt 15:21-28). For though my flesh and my heart may fail, "God is the strength of my heart and my portion forever" (Ps 73:26). What is there left to do at times but take and eat, together? And try, with all we are, in him, to re-member.

Manna: the gift of the present. Christ: the presence of his grace. I am beginning to see how the ultimate manna is Easter, the body as bread given by the God-man for the life of every human, everlasting. The manna, the Son of Man—this bread given for me—speaks of the provision, appropriateness and timeliness of God's love.

It is not necessary that I understand. The miracle of the mystery exists regardless. Though I am gently, thoroughly being loved into it.

Bowls and bowls of prayers pour over me like water—this sole washing, this cleansing of my soul, and with it, God's reminder that all that matters is that I am growing closer to him, that, as Psalm 73 sings, I trust I am entering his sanctuary, this Holy Place of the Present.

And I am. And it hurts. And it joys. And so I re-collect:

God's provision is in proportion.
And in his timing.
Through his heart
Then from his hand.

11

Living in the Presence

Who can say when or how it will be
that something easters up out of the dimness to remind us
of a time before we were born and after we will die?

FREDERICK BUECHNER

Sabbatum Sanctum.

Holy Saturday.

Sometimes called Black Saturday.

The day in the liturgical calendar when the altar is stripped bare. Mass is not held. Services are slivered, or silenced altogether.

Everything gets whittled down to a single point of light, or rather, to the dark in search of that nail hole of light. Everything emphasizes the essential.

Isn't this the startle into survival that all trauma, as embodied on the cross, brings?

Isn't this the devotion that sacrifice calls for, resulting in a clarity so bright it quiets?

We go silent on this Saturday, transported into the Holy Waiting.

We stay there, are held there. We remain in the Black. We, too, enter the tomb that becomes the womb. These are the still hours when the sun seems suspended.

No wonder Jesus visits hell between these two points.[1] The agony of waiting, of calling and yearning for a response, of grasping for the light switch of a promise kept in the complete dark. The seeming lack of movement from crucifixion to the resurrection, from the death of self into eternal life. A fear of the vague drifting of having turned away from the knowledge of God, and the perception of God's having turned away in return. What the ancients identified as the worst fate imaginable: the curse of having been forgotten.

Into the Black . . .

Going blind would be certainly difficult under any circumstances. But it seems especially tragic for someone who has dedicated his life to reading and writing. This is what happened to the seventeenth-century writer John Milton. He eventually composed much of his famous epic poem on the fall of humankind, *Paradise Lost*, blind. Legend has it that he dictated lines to his daughters, who acted as his scribes. And yet again we witness how trauma precedes resurrection. For as his eyesight flickered and waned, Milton would write a sonnet about seeing his loss in a different light, and in doing so, would give his reader a new vision of service before God as well. The poem's final line reads "They also serve who only stand and wait."[2]

Patience. Trust. Expectation. As Milton reminds us, these, too, are service. This stillness, more than restlessness, is faith.

But more often than not, I pace. Again, the slightest and yet greatest distinction between pace and peace.

Today I go for a walk because there is nothing else I can do. Kent and I feel as though we are waiting in the dark, caught in the concerns and nonanswers of the troubling prenatal tests for this treasured baby thus far. More than likely, our child will not be "normal," we have been informed repeatedly. We should prepare our-selves for the worst, the genetics counselors tell us. *Just what is this "worst"?* I find myself wondering. *Does this worst lie in the unborn child, in God—or in me?*

I can be still, or I can move. And so I choose to move, though it is a movement that does not take me anywhere. Forward and back, often it feels like steps to nowhere at all. *Sabbatum Sanctum* movement: rocking. The rock has moved in front of the tomb, and it cannot be moved without the help of heavenly hosts. For now, I am at the place where the rock closes up the window into wonder, eclipses my hope. I cannot see in. The angels are not here yet. So I walk away, like so many of those first believers did, too. Until those who *saw* and were found, ran to get those who wandered and were lost.

One of my favorite walks involves treading along the margin of the bean field that stretches out behind our local campus. It follows an extension of where I usually stop to survey the field in search of deer. Because the farmland originally belonged to a Catholic college, and still hosts a monastery, the Stations of the Cross originally used to line the rustic walk. Years later, only the station of the crucifixion remains. Though veined with cracks and worn with age, the monu-ment is still strikingly beautiful. Its white stone stands out in stark contrast to the surrounding brown brambles and shrubbery.

In my prayer walk from crowned child at the college gate to cru-cifix in the far-off field, I slowly gain my traction. I pound out my spiritual footing. I re-member my being. I come to squint at what is dear. To bring it back into focus. And in doing so, to protect what is precious.

Today, on this in-between of all days, I follow the same walk, the same path toward "the dear" that I have trod countless times before with the intent of traveling down into the valley, this time, however, all the way to the crucifix gleaming among the brambles. I cannot always enter the valley, as it poses a longer and sometimes impossibly muddy or icy walk; but today the trek seems particularly apt. So I wear boots for good measure and trade childcare time with my husband strategically to allow for this extension.

It is not an easy journey; the last part of the hike especially, overgrown and uneven, is not for the pilgrim faint of heart. The mud lies deep this time of year. In the months between, of stinging wind and frozen bough, the deer have not often emerged. I, too, ventured rarely, too cold and too discouraged by the icy path and stubbled fields to have my heart rent by what I feared from braving the plunge into murky dim-lit days: to be met with only a lack of the vision.

❁

A few weeks earlier, I had given a talk at a Toronto campus. Afterward, a student with a quiet but intense air startled me with the following question: *Is there such a thing as a "secular" world?*

I paused as the regular rhythms of my binary constructions hiccupped. The "either/ors" that have been so easy to fall into since Plato—nay, since Adam and Eve first transgressed in their reasoning that another truth must be better than God's truth.

In the second trimester of my pregnancy by then, I had started bleeding during my travels earlier that day. The amount was enough to be a cause for concern, but not enough to require canceling my commitment, I thought. After the dinner, the event, the discussion, the lingering group of students in conversation—I sneaked into the bathroom before walking back to the hotel. I was dismayed to find that the bleeding had grown notably worse, as had the discomfort. I reemerged, trying to conceal my anxiety.

My sister, however, knows me too well. One look at me and she hooked her arm through mine. "Come on," she whispered while looping me through a few remaining students (who would have, God bless students, talked with us until dawn if we had let them), "we're going to one of the hospitals on the way back to the hotel. It may be nothing or it may be something, but at the very least we'll gain some peace of mind."

I love my sister. Of the two of us, she is the pragmatic, sure-footed one. The one who sits up next to me all night in the waiting room, nodding from exhaustion. It was to be her first night away from her young children in some time as well. We had planned to share the drive together, then stay up late giggling in the hotel room after the talk, perhaps take a swim in the hotel pool, followed by eating enormous amounts of junk food before drifting off into slumber uninterrupted and then—luxury of all luxuries!—sleeping in late.

Instead, here it was 10 p.m., 11 p.m., midnight, then well into early morning—and we still sat huddled together, waiting for test results. Several times I tried sending her back to the hotel without me. It was only a block away.

"Go ahead, get some sleep," I urged. "I will be fine." I meant it. I was worried about her, too.

But she wouldn't hear of it. She wouldn't go.

We would finally return to the hotel with daybreak, tumbling into our beds for a few short hours of exhausted sleep before dragging ourselves out minutes before check-out time and drowsily entering into the concentration of a traffic-laden drive back.

Is this holy? Can this, too, be part of some meaning? Is there such a thing as a secular world?

"We cannot attain the presence of God because we are already totally in the presence of God," notes the Franciscan Richard Rohr.[3]

God's presence *is* everywhere, interfused through everything. This is not some loosey-goosey pantheistic observation. Rather, this is *Reality* when we choose to follow him, to live the life of abundance, which, contrary to other societal claims, truly is *abundant.*

However, I often have to remind myself that there really *is* enough to go around. More than enough. Far more than you or I could ever conceive of or measure. And it is Good. And it can be trusted. And though we are blind, or at best myopic, God is not. God is All. And so we are part of that vision and that light. Whether we know we are, or not. Or else the choice to believe would never even be there.

And yet what to make of this pilgrimage to and from a hospital, my sister's arm through mine, hurrying our way along damp streets amidst taxis and prostitutes and drunks? This trail of blood through a sleeping city under strips of stormy night sky?

A new life: so fragile. Such a gamble! Waiting to exhale, that's what pregnancy feels like. No wonder the mother-to-be is called expectant. In preceding centuries, pregnancy was referred to as "confinement." A woman had to stay close to home, or even hidden within the home, but even more so, she remained bound by the expectancy. Confined by the waiting, by the wavering wager between life and death, right up to the very last moment. Right up until delivery.

These tests in a different city only increased our original worry. Again, I was counseled to consider aborting. There certainly would be something "wrong" with the baby based on such protein levels, on such measurements from the ultrasounds—the list went on. The bleeding only added to our fears.

The question of the meaning of death is also the question of the meaning of life, the greatest of all questions. Death puts life into question. Cervantes's famous character Don Quixote addresses just this question when he tells Sancho Panza about the look he saw in the eyes of the soldiers who lay dying in his arms. The eyes seemed to be asking a question. Sancho asks, "Was it the question 'Why am I dying?'" to which Quixote replies, "No, it was the question 'Why was I living?'"[4]

"Life is always fatal. No one gets out of it alive," Peter Kreeft reminds us.[5] Thus, in order to live wisely, we must embrace the mystery and the meaning of death. By exploring facets of death, we define life, which brings us to the inevitable answer in the living God.

When I share across a great distance my concerns for this baby, my friend Charlene, an amazing wife, mother of nine and devout daughter of God, sends me a picture of her statue of the Pietà, encircled with candles she has lit in prayer for us. I stare at the breathtakingly beautiful image, all aglow. This visual, to me, perfectly represents birth-and-death. Mary cradles the Savior she birthed, the eternal made temporal, made complete in the God who endured death. She holds the body of the One who has become part of the "unchangeable, irreversible, closed past" so as to ensure for our spiritual bodies the eternal, free and abundant living.

"Remember," Charlene signs off her note, "Mary knows how you feel."

It is, indeed, finished, as Jesus declares in his last breath on the cross, his favorite disciple bearing witness. That same disciple would later close his letter on Revelation with Jesus' risen words, "Yes, I am coming soon" (22:20).

Finished. And yet . . . I remain cradling this question of death.

Come, Lord Jesus.

Come.

The Day of Preparation reminds me of how in our living we prepare to die. "At the place where Jesus was crucified, there was a garden, and in the garden a new tomb, in which no one had ever been laid. Because it was the Jewish day of Preparation and since the tomb was nearby, they laid Jesus there" (Jn 19:41-42).

Our sin in the first garden leads to our tomb in the second.

Whom would we want at our deathbed? It is more telling, I think, to consider not just with whom we would choose to live but with whom we would choose to die. Even if we reject him in life, do we not all long for Christ at our side in death? Is this hypocrisy, or merely humanity? As the old saying really does go, there is no such thing as an atheist in a foxhole. I believe with all I am that even the most diehard atheist carries a wisp of that innate cry, wrenched aloud or secreted deep inside, as the breath goes: *Come, Lord Jesus, come.*

I think of those with whom Jesus died, of those to whom he first revealed his risen being. Mary Magdalene, John tells us, in her weeping at the empty tomb mistook the risen Lord for a gardener. Such an interesting detail about mistaken identity: or is it mistaken? The Lord has returned as "first fruits" and will gather the harvest; he comes trailing the glory of the original garden, the very first calling of Adam. It is not until Jesus says her name that Mary recognizes who he is.

"May I never boast except in the cross of our Lord Jesus Christ, through which the world has been crucified to me, and I to the world" (Gal 6:14). Of course dying to ourselves and to the world is a form of trauma. All dying is. And we must allow for the mourning of the old to make clean way for "what counts," which is "the new creation" (Gal 6:15).

Love *is* stronger than death.

Tears are a passage from one world to another, from the broken to whole. Christianity is the only religion I have known that promises no tears in the restored world. Arriving at a place of healing and forgiveness, whether it be toward others or ourselves or both, brings this weepless peace. When I no longer feel the familiar pang of a past hurt, or when I search my heart but find that the spark of long-smoldering anger has been truly extinguished, I feel the drying of my eyes as though by some divine hand: a personal brush of my cheek that sweeps all the way to my soul. I breathe more deeply; the band around my heart has been loosed. And this small but mighty restoration, I wonder, must be a foretaste of life in the resurrected spiritual body. Like hearing my name called intimately by a nearby gardener who transforms before my very eyes into the living God, and who then sweeps me up as well in the transformation.

When Simon Peter entered the empty tomb, "he saw the strips of linen lying there, as well as the burial cloth that had been around Jesus' head. The cloth was folded up by itself, separate from the linen" (Jn 20:6-7 NIV 1984).[6] Perhaps because I am the keeper of a perpetually messy house, I am astounded by God's meticulousness in the folding of his burial cloth, especially given the circumstances—or perhaps exactly because of the circumstances? This is a beautiful example of how our Lord lurks in the details: clearly, we are shown, he has a plan and is in control. The folding of death clothes, the sign of preparing to put them away, itself becomes another act of care, of endurance, of love, even from deep within the tomb, the darkest of dark.

An ordinary gesture of an extraordinary verity: love is stronger than death.

It is okay to love deeply, the seen or the unseen. Even if this love comes with fear. For surely it will. I can't think of a love that is worth its salt unaccompanied by any fear at all. But it is in the facing of the fear and loving still, and through it, that the loving becomes burnished to a precious sheen and transformed into an ever-present gift.

Not to love as we are called to love is like living your life on the surface only: like coasting down an unspeakably beautiful scenic road while constantly riding your screeching brakes. Fear punctuates what should be run-on; it causes the song to catch in our throat. And yet it is the really deep love—the most fearsome—that carries us through life, death and into living again.

On this Holy Saturday, as I move among the trees, the baby moves inside of me. The sudden flutter causes me to think of how John the Baptist leaped in his mother's womb when Elizabeth met Mary, pregnant with our Lord. Is this how I meet my God—sight still unseen—from the very center of my expectancy? Is the miracle lessened at all by the threat of my worries? Or is the miracle in waiting, too—in my waiting, and in its own waiting, like a shoot coiled within the seed . . . faith meeting faith to heart-leap together?

Buds jewel the trees and the air hums with insects. The weather is in-between too, with a warmth singing of spring but a cool still edged with winter.

I have brought along the walking stick usually propped by our door. Today I need to lean on this emblem of knightly courage. The children found it months ago while walking in the woods by the creek, and although it is an entirely natural piece of wood, untouched by human artistry, its head appears carved into the shape of a dragon. I cherish it even more for its raw serendipity.

I choose the path along the water, too, and tap my stick as I go along, sometimes dragging lines in the damp earth behind me, sometimes tickling the close-lying vines and daffodils that bend over my path.

I stop as I approach the mouth of the path into the deeper woods.

This is the arch where the boughs will bend over me like a cathedral ceiling. I can see it with my eyes closed. Yes, even in the midst of bleakest winter, the scene rises up without effort: lush and green and thick and alive with every type of bud and flower, and birdsong so ornate you cannot make out a single tune.

Today, however, no traces of frost remain, and a seasonless sun hesitantly warms my face. The chatter and chortle of spring surround-sounds me, but it has not merged into full-throated song. The notes are still finding their way. I sense the buds moving toward bursting, but there are no blooms. All is expectant but not yet . . . not yet . . .

I prod some branches above me, perhaps trying to startle them into being. These are not speckled with green promise yet; instead they rattle like bare bones overhead, a vision fit for Ezekiel.

"Come, come!" I chide them, seeing that the snowdrops are poking through and the pussy willow is almost out. They do not answer but swing helplessly above me long after I have set down my stick. A slender, brittle arm snaps and falls to the ground.

I respond to their silence with silence. I lean against a fallen log, and the words loom up from the woods within me. I cannot help but think of "Nutting," written by the Romantic poet William Words-worth upon a similar excursion. The speaker of the poem recalls how as a child he once relentlessly rattled a tree to harvest its nuts. Remembering the pillage, the now adult voice realizes the violence he had so ignorantly done to nature and so turns to warn his sister: "Then, dearest Maiden! move along these shades / In gentleness of heart; with gentle hand / Touch,—for there is a spirit in the woods."[7]

There are times when this maiden doesn't want to be gentle of heart. I kick against being blessed. I want to shake "the tree." I want to rattle God's existence and make sure he is really there. I can be violent in such demands. One of a stiff-necked race, searing my gaze in one direction. Demanding that every need come from that direction to which I look. In my time, in my preference, in my sense of portion and propriety. I shake my stick. I urge him to rain down all I think I want, not what he knows I need.

All of my vehement efforts, all this noise, all of my shaking and moving for—and I couldn't help but smile at the pun from Wordsworth—*nuttin*.

The sacred wood lies all about us, in waiting, too.

.... ❀ ....

I stand amidst these spring-hungry trees and wonder: *What does it mean to be in God's presence?*

God does not remove his presence. Rather, we choose to step out from it.

What a longing, to return to this presence and know it, truly live it, for what it is! "To present you before his glorious presence" (Jude 1:24). For I know "you will fill me with joy in your presence" (Ps 16:11), the deep "rejoicing always in his presence" (Prov 8:30). And where two or more of us gather in praise and fellowship, we come together in the presence of God (Acts 10:33).

On this pilgrimage, I am learning some ways of stepping back in: to remember, to obey, to submit, to trust, to give thanks and to pray. Faithfulness calls to faithfulness; righteousness answers righteousness. For "God is present in the company of the righteous" (Ps 14:5), and "we set our hearts at rest in his presence" (1 John 3:19). Through the hole of the present, we see into the holy of the eternal. My decision in the now offers the keyhole to The Way.

Time and time again, the Bible illustrates that whenever we are out of God's presence we are cursed, reminded of our fallen condition and especially vulnerable to Satan's attack. "So Cain went out from the LORD's presence . . ." Genesis 4:16 tells us. The son who kills his brother rejects his God, and the result is exile. The Psalms acknowledge that "the arrogant cannot stand in your presence" (Ps 5:5) and pray, "Let the nations be judged in your presence" (Ps 9:19); even a king begs the True King to "be enthroned in God's presence forever" (Ps 61:7).

We see the effect of stepping away from God's presence in the very first story of all stories, when Adam and Eve move away from the direct presence of God and are seduced by the serpent. I used to ask myself: *why were Adam and Eve left alone when they ate the fruit—where was God?* They seem stranded in the heat of day when God comes shadily strolling in after the fact. But what if he had been there?

Surely God cannot be perpetually by our side, puppeteering our every move. Such a setup would suggest a controlling "Big Brother" more than a loving Father who honors trust and cultivates righteousness. As any good gardener knows, life thrives in light more than shadow. No, it is not that kind of presence—not an oppressive weight nor an ominous shadowing that follows our every move. Rather it is the "intangibility" of such things such as faith and obedience that are substance: substantive and substantial, bridging the gap between separated entities as "gold to airy thinness beat."[8]

While the righteous and the pure, such as the angels, stand in the presence of the Lord, the fallen and unredeemed cannot (Lk 1:19). For all of his power, and though he would desperately have us believe otherwise, Satan is rendered powerless in the face of God's authority. Even when he afflicted Job in probably one of the most extreme cases of suffering in the Bible, "Satan went out from the presence of the LORD" to do so (Job 1:12). Evil cannot afflict in the direct presence of God. Martyrs, saints, Christ himself show us that evil holds no power in the moment for those who hold fast to God.

And it certainly holds no power in eternity. "The humans live in time but our Enemy [God] destines them for eternity," C. S. Lewis's demonic character Screwtape reminds his protégé. One of the devil's slipperiest tricks to get us to lose our footing is to lure us to forget this doubled dignity.[9]

The first cry to our souls to follow our Lord brings us into his presence—or rather, shows us that it has never left us, only we it. Subsequent callings, however, fine-tune the pitch of the voice in our hearts. They open us wider into a more regular way of being attuned to God's voice in our lives, until callings become not unique happenings but a way of listening, a way of healing.

Door upon door opens up through the gate of the beautiful, into the pathway of miracles, this way.

✺

I began this book with the story about how my twins were born and the pivotal moment offered in my faith walk when my son and I faced possible death. The shout "Convert!" from my doctor in that operating room had shaken my first conversion to the core and threw into sharp relief the need to keep converting, to keep turning toward God.

I bring the book toward a close now with the story of another birth-to-be: a quiet act of hope. I do not know how this story will end. But I know how the larger one, the all-encompassing one, will. Well over a century after Hannah Whitall Smith wrote this, her wisdom endures:

But this faith of which I am speaking must be a present faith. No faith that is exercised in the future tense amounts to anything. A man may believe forever that his sins will be forgiven at some future time, and he will never find peace. He has to come to the *now* belief and say by faith, "My sins are now forgiven," before he can know the new birth.

Similarly, no faith which looks for a future deliverance from the power of sin will ever lead a soul into the life we are describing. Satan delights in this future faith, for he knows its powerlessness to accomplish any practical results. But he trembles and flees when the soul of the believer dares to claim a present deliverance, and to reckon itself now to be free from his power.[10]

Jesus stops the mouth of evil with his reply of prophecy fulfilled, promises kept. He did not stall at the Last Supper; he did not tarry at the tomb. Rather, he enacted his present in the ever-presence of grace. And, by extension, this is the power he has given us, every single moment of every single day (and night) that we live in him.

The darkness continues in the corner of this broken world. It has since the Fall and it will until the Return. As it did in that delivery room for me, as it does in that metaphorical place of deliverance for all of us: that passage of blood and water and flame and life and death . . .

But the darkness is always cornered. And eventually, it is not what endures. Evil cannot create but only destroy. Therefore I must keep trying to trust in the creation around me, within me. In myself as a new creation.

I take my manna with me, my portion for the moment: this daily bread. The Lord reigns over technology, too, no matter how self-sufficient and clever we like to think ourselves, so I carry my cell phone like a pocket-sized psalter, armed with support from my prayer circle. Prayers pour in from our pastor, fellow church members, friends in Christ far and wide—all close in him. All filling my bowl. The church results when two or more are gathered in him, even in e-space. Reverence is always relevant.

Scripture, fellowship, prayer: the manna that endures. For instance, when I ask my dear friend Pilar for prayer from within the darkness, at a moment when I am afraid that the corner will subsume the room, her words flash across the screen in my palm with perfect timeliness: "We are indestructible until God calls us home, Caro. God is BIG and He is in control of you, your life, and your baby . . . let us agree to stand in faith, let us continue to pray and believe . . . God says we only need a mustard seed of faith."[11]

We are indestructible until God calls us home.

And then? These still days illuminate the still: when we believe in him, we remain indestructible. We will abide, eternally, in him. Death is not all, but when we believe, it is a step toward All.

This day, I face the pilgrimage toward the Holy again. Into the dark. But perhaps the holy and the dark are not as disparate as they seem? Sometimes the holiest things come from the darkest, the blackest of holes, as George MacDonald notes in his poem "Lost and Found":

> I missed him when the sun began to bend;
> I found him not when I had lost his rim;
> With many tears I went in search of him,
> Climbing high mountains which did still ascend,
> And gave me echoes when I called my friend;
> Through cities vast and charnel-houses grim,
> And high cathedrals where the light was dim,
> Through books and arts and works without an end,
> But found him not—the friend whom I had lost.
> And yet I found him—as I found the lark,

A sound in fields I heard but could not mark;
I found him nearest when I missed him most;
I found him in my heart, a life in frost,
A light I knew not till my soul was dark.[12]

I choose my steps carefully along the muddied path. No roses here, only thorny patches. Now that I'm very pregnant, the difficult trail further challenges my balance. My feet catch in brambles, on knotted and gnarled roots coming up from the damp earth like the limbs of partially submerged sea monsters. I slip and teeter, and am forced to slow down. Alone in the briar far from any who could hear my call, I would not deem this a good time to fall.

Hitherto I have always pushed through, an attitude that tends to be my modus operandi but that can also be my illusionary self-sufficient undoing. With God, however, I'm learning how to be discerning, how to be care-full without being full of fear. The snags catch and tear, but I trust somehow I will reach the rose.

There are days through which we must go gently. Sometimes, entire life seasons. For how do we know what is as a day to the Lord? I am learning this now—a slow quickening. I am but a babe in him, but I am stretching within. Like a seed deep within the ground. These holy days are teaching me thus.

Suddenly, white flashes through bramble. A few steps more and I stand at the base of the statue of the crucifixion. You would not even know the breathtaking revelation broke here, unless you followed the path to its very end and then bent through the narrow bower.

I am not alone.

I think I shall see the scene in my soul's eye for as long as I live. After all my noisy, sole-sucking tramping through the muddy spring mush, I couldn't believe I hadn't frightened them away (nor spied them earlier). I was so caught up in my stomping down the path that I didn't notice what encompassed me.

And then the hush! The holy suspension of it all . . .

At the foot of the cross, literally, here, I realize I am surrounded by the "dear."

This time they are not specters of a far-off vision. They do not merely dot my vista, brown moving slightly against green from a safe distance, for both of us.

Rather, now they surround me, so close I could touch several of them if I leaned out, even just a little. A thrill runs through my body: not of danger, but of trust. It runs like a current, vivifying everything present, shocking all into gift.

The deer stand unperturbed except for tails gently swishing. They study me with bright eyes. I return the stare, blinking in belief.

We look upon each other, suspended in *kairos*. In God Time. In the Enough Time. In the stillness that speaks I AM THAT I AM.

Kairos.

Caro.

Dear one.

I breathe in the dear. There is no hunt this time. Rather, it has happened, *is happening.* I stand in their midst, awe-filled. In this broken world I am surrounded by pieces of him, and so I am surrounded by his peace. He gifts us with his presence, with his grace, in every moment we choose to be gifted, graced. The joy, though it surprises, has somehow been made complete in the choosing.

And the wonder of it! That something—some spirit, some, well, *Holy Spirit,* if I am to be mysteriously exact—precedes the knowledge that I will choose. That I have chosen, and been chosen. And so I will it, but it is willed. And like light and dark, sacred and secular, the two really aren't as incompatible as those generations trod and trod by philosophical debate would have it seem.

The body given in remembrance of God's love for us. The eternal made not only tangible and sustaining, but palatable and pleasing: true transubstantiation of the Real Presence. This *is* the bread of the presence: the dessert in my desert. This is the gift of the present given by the ultimate God-man for the resurrection of every human. The only bread by which we eat and live on and on, choosing and chosen of God.

Those of us who seek *carpe Deum* celebrate living in this holy waiting. The pilgrimage is one of anticipation and trust, where sorrow and suffering exist, but they cannot steal our joy, they cannot break the assurance, no matter how shredded or torn, of restoration beyond comprehension.

The deer bow their heads and graze on patches of burgeoning green. The trees creak and groan as the wind rushes above. There is no foliage yet to cushion such sounds of brittle anguish, no full-blown leaves to rustle and dance and roar like the sea. Yet not a single deer startles or bounds as I thread my way back toward the college, which sits like a castle at the crest of the hill with its ribbon of road stretching behind. Tiny purple flowers speckle the margin of my path. Just a few—but, somehow, enough.

In this sacred wood, I sense the seeding: the promise of verdancy, the presence of verity. "Blessed are those who wash their robes, that they may have the right to the tree of life and may go through the gates into the city" (Rev 22:14). Baptism marks the beginning of practicing our presence in him, this preparation for abundant living. Moment to moment, trusting his presence in, his love for, each of us is enough. For, Jesus reminds us, "surely I am with you always, to the very end of the age" (Mt 28:20).

Yes, he remains with us. Through negative and positive tests. Through what we think is loss, and what we hope is gain. Through a glass darkly. Through rocks rolled in front of our doorways. Through wounds and opportunities and wombs and tombs. Through days and nights and weekends and workdays. Through parking lots and hospitals and classrooms and communities. Through poverty and wealth and those who seek to believe and those who do not. Through the harshest of nows to the most glorious of always.

The shout on Palm Sunday heralds what we continue to shout through this current and cracked world of ours—this Time that stretches out as an extension of Holy Saturday until he comes again:

Hosanna!

The shortest psalm. The single-worded prayer that says it all. In Hebrew, the same phrase for "Help!" and "Praise!" The threshold, liminal place where dark and light, secular and sacred, willed and willing, almost imperceptibly meet.

God answers with his presence. In private thoughts and public crowds; in homes and prisons; in garden and on hill, sea, trial and cross . . .

He lives among us, often undetected, until we ask where he has gone.

And then he calls us by name. And we *see.*

The shared vision of such mutual calling. The intimacy of the presence of names. The grace of the private thought instilled in the salvation of a name only he knows and will reveal, to each of us, personally: "To the one who is victorious, I will give some of the hidden manna. I will also give that person a white stone with a new name written on it, known only to the one who receives it" (Rev 2:17).

Emmanuel.

God is with us.

Hidden manna, revealed.

The tremendous grace of the present.

I stand amidst budding trees brushing sky, the wind growing as the light is dying. And on this Easter eve, I know the death means only a brighter birth.

The baby quickens within me as I walk slowly home.

Notes

Chapter 2: The Widow's Offering

[1]T. S. Eliot, *The Cocktail Party* (Orlando, FL: Harcourt, 1950).

[2]Kathleen Norris, *Amazing Grace: A Vocabulary of Faith* (New York: Riverhead Books, 1998), p. 71.

[3]Ibid., p. 91.

[4]Tom Stoppard, *Arcadia* (London: Faber, 1993).

[5]John Berger, *Once in Europa* (New York: Pantheon, 1988), p. 39.

[6]Mary Poplin, *Finding Calcutta: What Mother Teresa Taught Me About Meaningful Work and Service* (Downers Grove, IL: InterVarsity Press, 2008), p. 148.

[7]George Steiner, *Real Presences* (London: Faber, 1989), p. 1.

[8]Edmund Vance Cooke, "The Spirit of the Gift."

Chapter 3: Refined like Silver

[1]Walter de la Mare, "Silver," in *Prose and Poetry of England*, ed. Julian L. Maline et al. (Syracuse, NY: L. W. Singer, 1949), p. 691.

[2]Author unknown, www.clarion-call.org/extras/malachi.htm.

[3]Brennan Manning, *The Ragamuffin Gospel* (Colorado Springs: Multnomah Books, 1990, rpt. 2005), p. 99.

[4]Ibid.

[5]C. S. Lewis, *Till We Have Faces: A Myth Retold* (New York: Harcourt, 1956), p. 306.

[6]Ibid., p. 308.

Chapter 4: U-Turn Friends

[1]John Milton, *Paradise Lost* (New York: W. W. Norton, 2005), bk. 1, lines 258-63.

[2]http://thinkexist.com/quotation/i_believe_in_person_to_person-every_person_is/149749.html.

[3]C. S. Lewis, "The Weight of Glory," in *Christian Reflections*, ed. Walter Hooper (Grand Rapids: Eerdmans, 1982), p. x.

Chapter 5: Even Jesus Went Out in a Boat

[1]Juliet Benner, *Contemplative Vision: A Guide to Christian Art and Prayer* (Downers Grove, IL: InterVarsity Press, 2011), p. 84.

Chapter 6: *Carpe Deum*

[1]Ann Schultz, "Carpe Diem," in *Message in a Bottle* (Rochester, MN: Artpacks, 2010), p. 5.

[2]Robert Herrick, "To the Virgins, to Make Much of Time," in *The Norton Anthology of English Literature*, ed. M. H. Abrams, 7th ed. (New York: W. W. Norton, 2000), 1:1649-50.

[3]Thomas Traherne, quoted in Madeleine L'Engle, *Walking on Water: Reflections on Faith and Art* (New York: North Point Press, 1995), p. 102.

[4]Thomas Merton, quoted in Kathleen Norris, *Amazing Grace: A Vocabulary of Faith* (New York: Riverhead Books, 1998) p. 108.

[5]Anne Lamott, *Traveling Mercies: Some Thoughts on Faith* (New York: Anchor Books, 2001), p. 168.

[6]Emily Dickinson, *Letters of Emily Dickinson*, ed. Thomas Johnson and Theodora Ward (Cambridge, MA: Belknap Press of Harvard University Press, 1958), p. 178.

[7]*Newsweek* interview with Madeleine L'Engle, May 6, 2004, available at www.thedaily beast.com/newsweek/2004/05/06/i-dare-you.html.

Chapter 7: Exclamation Marks in the Sky!

[1]Jean-Pierre de Caussade, *The Sacrament of the Present Moment* (San Francisco: Harper, 1978), p. 80.

[2]Ken Gire, *Seeing What Is Sacred* (Nashville: Thomas Nelson, 2006), pp. 90-91.

[3]Ann Voskamp, *One Thousand Gifts* (Grand Rapids: Zondervan, 2010), p. 132.

[4]Madeleine L'Engle, *The Rock That Is Higher: Story as Truth* (Wheaton, IL: Harold Shaw, 1993), p. 214.

[5]Anne Morrow Lindbergh, *Gift from the Sea* (New York: Pantheon Books, 1955, rpt. 2005), pp. 97-98.

[6]Craig Groeschel, *Weird: Because Normal Isn't Working* (Grand Rapids: Zondervan, 2011).

[7]Henri Cormier, *The Humor of Jesus* (New York: Alba House, 1977), pp. 66-67.

Chapter 8: At the Threshold

[1]George MacDonald, "Obedience," in *The World's Great Religious Poetry*, ed. Caroline Miles Hill (New York: Macmillan, 1936), p. 632.

[2]Kathleen Norris, *Amazing Grace: A Vocabulary of Faith* (New York: Riverhead Books, 1998), pp. 146-47.

[3]Anne Lamott, *Plan B: Further Thoughts on Faith* (New York: Riverhead Books, 2005), p. 66.

[4]Henry Drummond, *The Greatest Thing in the World* (Grand Rapids: Baker Books, 2011), pp. 51-52.

Chapter 9: The Dear Hunt

[1]William Blake, "The Sick Rose," in *The Norton Anthology of Literature*, 8th ed., vol. D (New York and London: Norton, 2006), p. 91.

[2]Leslie Leyland Fields, *Surviving the Island of Grace* (Kenmore, WA: Epicenter, 2008), p. 245.

[3]I extend my gratitude to Pastor Jon Korkidakis of Village Green Community Church in London, Canada, for his usual wisdom.

[4]Dorothy Sayers, *The Mind of the Maker* (orig. 1941; San Francisco: HarperCollins, 1979), p. 49.

Chapter 10: Grumble and Trust

[1]Milan Kundera, *The Unbearable Lightness of Being* (New York: HarperCollins, 1991), p. 11.

[2]Charles Swindoll, *New Testament Insights: Revelation* (Grand Rapids: Zondervan, 2011), p. 250.

[3]Roger Pooley, "What Does Literature Do?" in *The Discerning Reader: Christian Perspectives on Criticism and Theory*, ed. David Barratt, Roger Pooley and Leland Ryken (Grand Rapids: Baker Books, 1995), p. 28.

[4]Dietrich Bonhoeffer, *Reflections on the Bible* (Peabody, MA: Hendrickson, 2004), p. 31.

[5]Frederick Buechner, *Telling the Truth: The Gospel as Tragedy, Comedy and Fairy Tale* (New York: HarperCollins, 1977), p. 98.

Chapter 11: Living in the Presence

[1]See, for instance, the Apostles' and Athanasian Creeds.

[2]John Milton, "Sonnet on His Blindness," in *The World's Great Religious Poetry*, ed. Caroline Miles Hill (New York: Macmillan, 1936), p. 597.

[3]Richard Rohr, *Everything Belongs: The Gift of Contemplative Prayer*, rev. ed. (New York: Crossroad, 2003).

[4]Quoted in Peter Kreeft, *Love Is Stronger Than Death* (San Francisco: Ignatius, 1992), p. xvi.

[5]Ibid., p. xv.

[6]The 2011 NIV reads, "The cloth was still lying in its place, separate from the linen," though many other translations describe the cloth as folded or rolled. The detail stands that the head wrap is put aside carefully; there is a plan, something deliberate.

[7]William Wordsworth, "Nutting," in *Lyrical Ballads*, ed. R. L. Brett and A. R. Jones, 2nd ed. (London: Routledge, 1991), pp. 196-98.

[8]I am borrowing John Donne's beautiful analogy from his poem "A Valediction Forbidding Mourning."

[9]C. S. Lewis, *The Screwtape Letters* (New York: Macmillan, 1982).

[10]Hannah Whitall Smith, *The Christian's Secret of a Happy Life* (Berkeley, CA: Apocryphal, 2007), p. 14.

[11]In a note from dear friend Pilar Arsenac, April 6, 2012.

[12]George MacDonald, "Lost and Found," in *The World's Great Religious Poetry*, p. 39.